RHETOR
BY

Aristotle

Translated by Theodorus Gaza

Rhetoric

BOOK I

Part 1

1. Rhetoric is a counterpart of Dialectic; for both have to do with matters that are in a manner within the cognizance of all men and not confined to any special science. Hence all men in a manner have a share of both; for all, up to a certain point, endeavor to criticize or uphold an argument, to defend themselves or to accuse. [2] Now, the majority of people do this either at random or with a familiarity arising from habit. But since both these ways are possible, it is clear that matters can be reduced to a system, for it is possible to examine the reason why some attain their end by familiarity and others by chance; and such an examination all would at once admit to be the function of an art.

[3] Now, previous compilers of "Arts" of Rhetoric have provided us with only a small portion of this art, for proofs are the only things in it that come within the province of art; everything else is merely an accessory. And yet they say nothing about enthymemes which are the body of proof, but chiefly devote their attention to matters outside the subject; [4] for the arousing of prejudice, compassion, anger, and similar emotions has no connection with the matter in hand, but is directed only to the dicast. The result would be that, if all trials were now carried on as they are in some States,
especially those that are well administered, there would be nothing left for the rhetorician to say. [5] For all men either think that all the laws ought so to prescribe, or in fact carry out the principle and forbid speaking outside the subject, as in the court of Areopagus, and in this they are right. For it is wrong to warp the dicast's feelings, to arouse him to anger, jealousy or compassion, which would be like making the rule crooked which one intended to use. [6] Further, it is evident that the only business of the litigant is to prove that the fact in question is or is not so, that it has happened or not; whether it is important or unimportant, just or unjust, in all cases in which the legislator has not laid down a ruling, is a matter for the dicast himself to decide; it is not the business of the litigants to instruct him.

[7] First of all, therefore, it is proper that laws, properly enacted, should themselves define the issue of all cases as far as possible, and leave as little as possible to the discretion of the judges; in the first place, because it is easier to find one or a few men of good sense,
capable of framing laws and pronouncing judgements, than a large number; secondly, legislation is the result of long consideration, whereas judgements are delivered on the spur of the moment, so that it is difficult for the judges properly to decide questions of justice or expediency. But what is most important of all is that the judgement of the legislator does not apply to a particular

case, but is universal and applies to the future, whereas the member of the public assembly and the dicast have to decide present and definite issues, and in their case love, hate, or personal interest is often involved, so that they are no longer capable of discerning the truth adequately, their judgement being obscured by their own pleasure or pain.

[8] All other cases, as we have just said, should be left to the authority of the judge as seldom as possible, except where it is a question of a thing having happened or not, of its going to happen or not, of being or not being so; this must be left to the discretion of the judges, for it is impossible for the legislator to foresee such questions. [9] If this is so, it is obvious that all those who definitely lay down, for instance, what should be the contents of the exordium or the narrative, or of the other parts of the discourse, are bringing under the rules of art what is outside the subject; for the only thing to which their attention is devoted
is how to put the judge into a certain frame of mind. They give no account of the artificial proofs, which make a man a master of rhetorical argument.

[10] Hence, although the method of deliberative and forensic Rhetoric is the same, and although the pursuit of the former is nobler and more worthy of a statesman than that of the latter, which is limited to transactions between private citizens, they say nothing about the former, but without exception endeavor to bring forensic speaking under the rules of art. The reason of this is that in public speaking it is less worth while to talk of what is outside the subject, and that deliberative oratory lends itself to trickery less than forensic, because it is of more general interest. For in the assembly the judges decide upon their own affairs, so that the only thing necessary is to prove the truth of the statement of one who recommends a measure, but in the law courts this is not sufficient; there it is useful to win over the hearers, for the decision concerns other interests than those of the judges, who, having only themselves to consider and listening merely for their own pleasure, surrender to the pleaders but do not give a real decision.
That is why, as I have said before, in many places the law prohibits speaking outside the subject in the law courts, whereas in the assembly the judges themselves take adequate precautions against this.

[11] It is obvious, therefore, that a system arranged according to the rules of art is only concerned with proofs; that proof is a sort of demonstration, since we are most strongly convinced when we suppose anything to have been demonstrated; that rhetorical demonstration is an enthymeme, which, generally speaking, is the strongest of rhetorical proofs and lastly, that the enthymeme is a kind of syllogism. Now, as it is the function of Dialectic as a whole, or of one of its parts, to consider every kind of syllogism in a similar manner, it is clear that he who is most capable of examining the matter and forms of a syllogism will be in the highest degree a master of rhetorical argument, if to this he adds a knowledge of the subjects with which enthymemes deal and the differences between them and logical syllogisms. For, in fact, the true and that which resembles it come under the purview of the same faculty, and at the same time men have a sufficient natural capacity for the truth and indeed in most cases attain to it; wherefore one who divines well in regard to the truth will also be able to divine well in regard to probabilities.

It is clear, then, that all other rhetoricians bring under the rules of art what is outside the subject, and have rather inclined to the forensic branch of oratory. [12] Nevertheless, Rhetoric is useful,

because the true and the just are naturally superior to their opposites, so that, if decisions are improperly made, they must owe their defeat to their own advocates; which is reprehensible. Further, in dealing with certain persons, even if we possessed the most accurate scientific knowledge, we should not find it easy to persuade them by the employment of such knowledge. For scientific discourse is concerned with instruction, but in the case of such persons instruction is impossible; our proofs and arguments must rest on generally accepted principles, as we said in the Topics, when speaking of converse with the multitude. Further, the orator should be able to prove opposites, as in logical arguments; not that we should do both （for one ought not to persuade people to do what is wrong）, but that the real state of the case may not escape us, and that we ourselves may be able to counteract false arguments, if another makes an unfair use of them. Rhetoric and Dialectic alone of all the arts prove opposites; for both are equally concerned with them. However, it is not the same with the subject matter, but, generally speaking, that which is true and better is naturally always easier to prove and more likely to persuade. Besides, it would be absurd if it were considered disgraceful not to be able to defend oneself with the help of the body,
but not disgraceful as far as speech is concerned, whose use is more characteristic of man than that of the body. [13] If it is argued that one who makes an unfair use of such faculty of speech may do a great deal of harm, this objection applies equally to all good things except virtue, and above all to those things which are most useful, such as strength, health, wealth, generalship; for as these, rightly used, may be of the greatest benefit, so, wrongly used, they may do an equal amount of harm.

[14] It is thus evident that Rhetoric does not deal with any one definite class of subjects, but, like Dialectic, [is of general application]; also, that it is useful; and further, that its function is not so much to persuade, as to find out in each case the existing means of persuasion. The same holds good in respect to all the other arts. For instance, it is not the function of medicine to restore a patient to health, but only to promote this end as far as possible; for even those whose recovery is impossible may be properly treated. It is further evident that it belongs to Rhetoric to discover the real and apparent means of persuasion, just as it belongs to Dialectic to discover the real and apparent syllogism. For what makes the sophist is not the faculty but the moral purpose. But there is a difference: in Rhetoric, one who acts in accordance with sound argument, and one who acts in accordance with moral purpose,
are both called rhetoricians; but in Dialectic it is the moral purpose that makes the sophist, the dialectician being one whose arguments rest, not on moral purpose but on the faculty.

Let us now endeavor to treat of the method itself, to see how and by what means we shall be able to attain our objects. And so let us as it were start again, and having defined Rhetoric anew, pass on to the remainder of the subject.

Part 2

2. Rhetoric then may be defined as the faculty of discovering the possible means of persuasion in reference to any subject whatever. This is the function of no other of the arts, each of which is able to instruct and persuade in its own special subject; thus, medicine deals with health and sickness, geometry with the properties of magnitudes, arithmetic with number, and similarly with all the other arts and sciences. But Rhetoric, so to say, appears to be able to discover the means of persuasion in reference to any given subject. That is why we say that as an art its rules are not applied to any particular definite class of things.

[2] As for proofs, some are artificial, others inartificial. By the latter I understand all those which have not been furnished by ourselves but were already in existence, such as witnesses, tortures, contracts, and the like; by the former, all that can be constructed by system and by our own efforts. Thus we have only to make use of the latter, whereas we must invent the former.

[3] Now the proofs furnished by the speech are of three kinds. The first depends upon the moral character of the speaker, the second upon putting the hearer into a certain frame of mind, the third upon the speech itself, in so far as it proves or seems to prove.

[4] The orator persuades by moral character when his speech is delivered in such a manner as to render him worthy of confidence; for we feel confidence in a greater degree and more readily in persons of worth in regard to everything in general, but where there is no certainty and there is room for doubt, our confidence is absolute. But this confidence must be due to the speech itself, not to any preconceived idea of the speaker's character; for it is not the case, as some writers of rhetorical treatises lay down in their "Art," that the worth of the orator in no way contributes to his powers of persuasion; on the contrary, moral character, so to say, constitutes the most effective means of proof. [5] The orator persuades by means of his hearers, when they are roused to emotion by his speech; for the judgements we deliver are not the same when we are influenced by joy or sorrow, love or hate; and it is to this alone that, as we have said, the present-day writers of treatises endeavor to devote their attention. (We will discuss these matters in detail when we come to speak of the emotions.) [6] Lastly, persuasion is produced by the speech itself, when we establish the true
or apparently true from the means of persuasion applicable to each individual subject.

[7] Now, since proofs are effected by these means, it is evident that, to be able to grasp them, a man must be capable of logical reasoning, of studying characters and the virtues, and thirdly the emotions—the nature and character of each, its origin, and the manner in which it is produced. Thus it appears that Rhetoric is as it were an offshoot of Dialectic and of the science of Ethics, which may be reasonably called Politics. That is why Rhetoric assumes the character of Politics, and those who claim to possess it, partly from ignorance, partly from boastfulness, and partly from other human weaknesses, do the same. For, as we said at the outset, Rhetoric is a sort of division or likeness of Dialectic, since neither of them is a science that deals with the nature of any definite subject, but they are merely faculties of furnishing arguments. We have now said nearly enough about the faculties of these arts and their mutual relations.

[8] But for purposes of demonstration, real or apparent, just as Dialectic possesses two modes of argument,
induction and the syllogism, real or apparent, the same is the case in Rhetoric; for the example is induction, and the enthymeme a syllogism, and the apparent enthymeme an apparent syllogism. Accordingly I call an enthymeme a rhetorical syllogism, and an example rhetorical induction. Now all orators produce belief by employing as proofs either examples or enthymemes and nothing else; so that if, generally speaking, it is necessary to prove any fact whatever either by syllogism or by induction—and that this is so is clear from the Analytics—each of the two former must be identical with each of the two latter. [9] The difference between example and enthymeme is evident from the Topics, where, in discussing syllogism and induction, it has previously been said that the proof from a number of particular cases that such is the rule, is called in Dialectic induction, in Rhetoric example; but when, certain things being posited, something different results by reason of them, alongside of them, from their being true, either universally or in most cases, such a conclusion in Dialectic is called a syllogism, in Rhetoric an enthymeme.

[10] It is evident that Rhetoric enjoys both these advantages—
for what has been said in the Methodica holds good also in this case—for rhetorical speeches are sometimes characterized by examples and sometimes by enthymemes, and orators themselves may be similarly distinguished by their fondness for one or the other. Now arguments that depend on examples are not less calculated to persuade, but those which depend upon enthymemes meet with greater approval. [11] Their origin and the way in which each should be used will be discussed later; for the moment let us define more clearly these proofs themselves.

Now, that which is persuasive is persuasive in reference to some one, and is persuasive and convincing either at once and in and by itself, or because it appears to be proved by propositions that are convincing; further, no art has the particular in view, medicine for instance what is good for Socrates or Callias, but what is good for this or that class of persons (for this is a matter that comes within the province of an art, whereas the particular is infinite and cannot be the subject of a true science; similarly, therefore, Rhetoric will not consider what seems probable in each individual case, for instance to Socrates or Hippias, but that which seems probable to this or that class of persons. It is the same with Dialectic, which does not draw conclusions from any random premises—for even madmen have some fancies—but it takes its material from subjects which demand reasoned discussion, as Rhetoric does from those which are common subjects of deliberation.

[12] The function of Rhetoric, then, is to deal with things about which we deliberate, but for which we have no systematic rules; and in the presence of such hearers as are unable to take a general view of many stages, or to follow a lengthy chain of argument. But we only deliberate about things which seem to admit of issuing in two ways; as for those things which cannot in the past, present, or future be otherwise, no one deliberates about them, if he supposes that they are such; for nothing would be gained by it. [13] Now, it is possible to draw conclusions and inferences partly from what has been previously demonstrated syllogistically, partly from what has not, which however needs demonstration, because it is not probable. The first of these methods is necessarily difficult to follow owing to its length, for the judge is supposed to be a simple person; the second will obtain little credence, because it does not depend upon what is

either admitted or probable. The necessary result then is that the enthymeme and the example are concerned with things which may, generally speaking, be other than they are, the example being a kind of induction and the enthymeme a kind of syllogism, and deduced from few premises, often from fewer than the regular syllogism; for if any one of these is well known, there is no need to mention it, for the hearer can add it himself. For instance, to prove that Dorieus was the victor in a contest at which the prize was a crown,

it is enough to say that he won a victory at the Olympic games; there is no need to add that the prize at the Olympic games is a crown, for everybody knows it.

[14] But since few of the propositions of the rhetorical syllogism are necessary, for most of the things which we judge and examine can be other than they are, human actions, which are the subject of our deliberation and examination, being all of such a character and, generally speaking, none of them necessary; since, further, facts which only generally happen or are merely possible can only be demonstrated by other facts of the same kind, and necessary facts by necessary propositions (and that this is so is clear from the <u>Analytics</u>, it is evident that the materials from which enthymemes are derived will be sometimes necessary, but for the most part only generally true; and these materials being probabilities and signs, it follows that these two elements must correspond to these two kinds of propositions, each to each. [15] For that which is probable is that which generally happens, not however unreservedly, as some define it, but that which is concerned with things that may be other than they are, being so related to that in regard to which it is probable

as the universal to the particular. [16] As to signs, some are related as the particular to the universal, others as the universal to the particular. Necessary signs are called tekmeria; those which are not necessary have no distinguishing name. [17] I call those necessary signs from which a logical syllogism can be constructed, wherefore such a sign is called tekmērion; for when people think that their arguments are irrefutable, they think that they are bringing forward a tekmērion, something as it were proved and concluded; for in the old language tekmar and peras have the same meaning (limit, conclusion) .

[18] Among signs, some are related as the particular to the universal; for instance, if one were to say that all wise men are just, because Socrates was both wise and just. Now this is a sign, but even though the particular statement is true, it can be refuted, because it cannot be reduced to syllogistic form. But if one were to say that it is a sign that a man is ill, because he has a fever, or that a woman has had a child because she has milk, this is a necessary sign. This alone among signs is a **tekmērion**; for only in this case, if the fact is true, is the argument irrefutable. Other signs are related as the universal to the particular, for instance, if one were to say that it is a sign that this man has a fever, because he breathes hard; but even if the fact be true, this argument also can be refuted, for it is possible for a man to breathe hard without having a fever. We have now explained the meaning of probable, sign, and necessary sign, and the difference between them; in the <u>Analytics</u> we have defined them more clearly and stated why some of them can be converted into logical syllogisms, while others cannot.

[19] We have said that example is a kind of induction and with what kind of material it deals by way of induction. It is neither the relation of part to whole, nor of whole to part, nor of one whole to another whole, but of part to part, of like to like, when both come under the same genus, but one of them is better known than the other. For example, to prove that Dionysius is aiming at a

tyranny, because he asks for a bodyguard, one might say that Pisistratus before him and Theagenes of <u>Megara</u> did the same, and when they obtained what they asked for made themselves tyrants. All the other tyrants known may serve as an example of Dionysius, whose reason, however, for asking for a bodyguard we do not yet know. All these examples are contained under the same universal proposition, that one who is aiming at a tyranny asks for a bodyguard.

We have now stated the materials of proofs which are thought to be demonstrative. [20] But a very great difference between enthymemes has escaped the notice of nearly every one, although it also exists in the dialectical method of syllogisms. For some of them belong to Rhetoric, some syllogisms only to Dialectic, and others to other arts and faculties, some already existing and others not yet established. Hence it is that this escapes the notice of the speakers, and the more they specialize in a subject, the more they transgress the limits of Rhetoric and Dialectic. But this will be clearer if stated at greater length.

[21] I mean by dialectical and rhetorical syllogisms those which are concerned with what we call "topics," which may be applied alike to Law, Physics, Politics, and many other sciences that differ in kind, such as the topic of the more or less, which will furnish syllogisms and enthymemes equally well for Law, Physics, or any other science whatever, although these subjects differ in kind. Specific topics on the other hand are derived from propositions which are peculiar to each species or genus of things; there are, for example, propositions about Physics which can furnish neither enthymemes nor syllogisms about Ethics,
and there are propositions concerned with Ethics which will be useless for furnishing conclusions about Physics; and the same holds good in all cases. The first kind of topics will not make a man practically wise about any particular class of things, because they do not deal with any particular subject matter; but as to the specific topics, the happier a man is in his choice of propositions, the more he will unconsciously produce a science quite different from Dialectic and Rhetoric. For if once he hits upon first principles, it will no longer be Dialectic or Rhetoric, but that science whose principles he has arrived at. [22] Most enthymemes are constructed from these specific topics, which are called particular and special, fewer from those that are common or universal. As then we have done in the <u>Topics</u>, so here we must distinguish the specific and universal topics, from which enthymemes may be constructed. By specific topics I mean the propositions peculiar to each class of things, by universal those common to all alike. Let us then first speak of the specific topics, but before doing so let us ascertain the different kinds of Rhetoric, so that, having determined their number, we may separately ascertain their elements and propositions.

Part 3

3. The kinds of Rhetoric are three in number, corresponding to the three kinds of hearers. For every speech is composed of three parts: the speaker,
the subject of which he treats, and the person to whom it is addressed, I mean the hearer, to

whom the end or object of the speech refers. [2] Now the hearer must necessarily be either a mere spectator or a judge, and a judge either of things past or of things to come. For instance, a member of the general assembly is a judge of things to come; the dicast, of things past; the mere spectator, of the ability of the speaker. [3] Therefore there are necessarily three kinds of rhetorical speeches, deliberative, forensic, and epideictic.

The deliberative kind is either hortatory or dissuasive; for both those who give advice in private and those who speak in the assembly invariably either exhort or dissuade. The forensic kind is either accusatory or defensive; for litigants must necessarily either accuse or defend. The epideictic kind has for its subject praise or blame.

[4] Further, to each of these a special time is appropriate: to the deliberative the future, for the speaker, whether he exhorts or dissuades, always advises about things to come; to the forensic the past, for it is always in reference to things done that one party accuses and the other defends; to the epideictic most appropriately the present, for it is the existing condition of things that all those who praise or blame have in view. It is not uncommon, however, for epideictic speakers to avail themselves of other times, of the past
by way of recalling it, or of the future by way of anticipating it.

[5] Each of the three kinds has a different special end, and as there are three kinds of Rhetoric, so there are three special ends. The end of the deliberative speaker Is the expedient or harmful; for he who exhorts recommends a course of action as better, and he who dissuades advises against it as worse; all other considerations, such as justice and injustice, honor and disgrace, are included as accessory in reference to this. The end of the forensic speaker is the just or the unjust; in this case also all other considerations are included as accessory. The end of those who praise or blame is the honorable and disgraceful; and they also refer all other considerations to these. [6] A sign that what I have stated is the end which each has in view is the fact that sometimes the speakers will not dispute about the other points. For example, a man on trial does not always deny that an act has been committed or damage inflicted by him, but he will never admit that the act is unjust; for otherwise a trial would be unnecessary. Similarly, the deliberative orator, although he often sacrifices everything else, will never admit that he is recommending what is inexpedient or is dissuading from what is useful; but often he is quite indifferent about showing that the enslavement of neighboring peoples, even if they have done no harm, is not an act of injustice. Similarly, those who praise or blame do not consider
whether a man has done what is expedient or harmful, but frequently make it a matter for praise that, disregarding his own interest, he performed some deed of honor. For example, they praise Achilles because he went to the aid of his comrade Patroclus, knowing that he was fated to die, although he might have lived. To him such a death was more honorable, although life was more expedient.

[7] From what has been said it is evident that the orator must first have in readiness the propositions on these three subjects. Now, necessary signs, probabilities, and signs are the propositions of the rhetorician; for the syllogism universally consists of propositions, and the enthymeme is a syllogism composed of the propositions above mentioned. [8] Again, since what is impossible can neither have been done nor will be done, but only what is possible, and since what has not taken place nor will take place can neither have been done nor will be done, it is

necessary for each of the three kinds of orators to have in readiness propositions dealing with the possible and the impossible, and as to whether anything has taken place or will take place, or not. [9] Further, since all, whether they praise or blame, exhort or dissuade, accuse or defend, not only endeavor to prove what we have stated, but also that the same things,
whether good or bad, honorable or disgraceful, just or unjust, are great or small, either in themselves or when compared with each other, it is clear that it will be necessary for the orator to be ready with propositions dealing with greatness and smallness and the greater and the less, both universally and in particular; for instance, which is the greater or less good, or act of injustice or justice; and similarly with regard to all other subjects. We have now stated the topics concerning which the orator must provide himself with propositions; after this, we must distinguish between each of them individually, that is, what the three kinds of Rhetoric, deliberative, epideictic, and forensic, are concerned with.

Part 4

4. We must first ascertain about what kind of good or bad things the deliberative orator advises, since he cannot do so about everything, but only about things which may possibly happen or not. [2] Everything which of necessity either is or will be, or which cannot possibly be or come to pass, is outside the scope of deliberation. [3] Indeed, even in the case of things that are possible advice is not universally appropriate; for they include certain advantages, natural and accidental, about which it is not worth while to offer advice. But it is clear that advice is limited to those subjects about which we take counsel; and such are all those which can naturally be referred to ourselves and the first cause of whose origination is in our own power;
for our examination is limited to finding out whether such things are possible or impossible for us to perform.

[4] However, there is no need at present to endeavor to enumerate with scrupulous exactness or to classify those subjects which men are wont to discuss, or to define them as far as possible with strict accuracy, since this is not the function of the rhetorical art but of one that is more intelligent and exact, and further, more than its legitimate subjects of inquiry have already been assigned to it. [5] For what we have said before is true: that Rhetoric is composed of analytical science and of that branch of political science which is concerned with Ethics, and that it resembles partly Dialectic and partly sophistical arguments. [6] But in proportion as anyone endeavors to make of Dialectic or Rhetoric, not what they are, faculties, but sciences, to that extent he will, without knowing it, destroy their real nature, in thus altering their character, by crossing over into the domain of sciences, whose subjects are certain definite things, not merely words. [7] Nevertheless, even at present we may mention such matters as it is worth while to analyze, while still leaving much for political science to investigate.

Now, we may say that the most important subjects about which all men deliberate and deliberative orators harangue, are five in number, to wit: ways and means, war and peace, the defence of the country, imports and exports, legislation.

[8] Accordingly, the orator who is going to give advice on ways and means should be acquainted with the nature and extent of the State resources, so that if any is omitted it may be added, and if

any is insufficient, it may be increased. Further, he should know all the expenses of the State, that if any is superfluous, it may be removed, or, if too great, may be curtailed. For men become wealthier, not only by adding to what they already possess, but also by cutting down expenses. Of these things it is not only possible to acquire a general view from individual experience, but in view of advising concerning them it is further necessary to be well informed about what has been discovered among others.

[9] In regard to war and peace, the orator should be acquainted with the power of the State, how great it is already and how great it may possibly become; of what kind it is already and what additions may possibly be made to it; further, what wars it has waged and its conduct of them. These things he should be acquainted with, not only as far as his own State is concerned, but also in reference to neighboring States, and particularly those with whom there is a likelihood of war, so that towards the stronger a pacific attitude may be maintained,
and in regard to the weaker, the decision as to making war on them may be left to his own State. Again, he should know whether their forces are like or unlike his own, for herein also advantage or disadvantage may lie. With reference to these matters he must also have examined the results, not only of the wars carried on by his own State, but also of those carried on by others; for similar results naturally arise from similar causes.

[10] Again, in regard to the defense of the country, he should not be ignorant how it is carried on; he should know both the strength of the guard, its character, and the positions of the guard-houses（which is impossible for one who is unacquainted with the country）, so that if any guard is insufficient it may be increased, or if any is superfluous it may be disbanded, and greater attention devoted to suitable positions.

[11] Again, in regard to food, he should know what amount of expenditure is sufficient to support the State; what kind of food is produced at home or can be imported; and what exports and imports are necessary, in order that contracts and agreements may be made with those who can furnish them; for it is necessary to keep the citizens free from reproach in their relations with two classes of people—those who are stronger and those who are useful for commercial purposes.

[12] With a view to the safety of the State, it is necessary that the orator should be able to judge of all these questions, but an understanding of legislation is of special importance, for it is on the laws
that the safety of the State is based. Wherefore he must know how many forms of government there are; what is expedient for each; and the natural causes of its downfall, whether they are peculiar to the particular form of government or opposed to it. By being ruined by causes peculiar to itself, I mean that, with the exception of the perfect form of government, all the rest are ruined by being relaxed or strained to excess. Thus democracy, not only when relaxed, but also when strained to excess, becomes weaker and will end in an oligarchy; similarly, not only does an aquiline or snub nose reach the mean, when one of these defects is relaxed, but when it becomes aquiline or snub to excess, it is altered to such an extent that even the likeness of a nose is lost. [13] Moreover, with reference to acts of legislation, it is useful not only to understand what form of government is expedient by judging in the light of the past, but also to become acquainted with those in existence in other nations, and to learn what kinds of government are

suitable to what kinds of people. It is clear, therefore, that for legislation books of travel are useful, since they help us to understand the laws of other nations, and for political debates historical works. All these things, however, belong to Politics and not to Rhetoric.

Such, then, are the most important questions upon which the would-be deliberative orator must be well informed. Now let us again state the sources whence we must derive our arguments for exhortation or discussion on these and other questions.

Part 5

5. Men, individually and in common, nearly all have some aim, in the attainment of which they choose or avoid certain things. This aim, briefly stated, is happiness and its component parts. [2] Therefore, for the sake of illustration, let us ascertain what happiness, generally speaking, is, and what its parts consist in; for all who exhort or dissuade discuss happiness and the things which conduce or are detrimental to it. For one should do the things which procure happiness or one of its parts, or increase instead of diminishing it, and avoid doing those things which destroy or hinder it or bring about what is contrary to it.

[3] Let us then define happiness as well-being combined with virtue, or independence of life, or the life that is most agreeable combined with security, or abundance of possessions and slaves, combined with power to protect and make use of them; for nearly all men admit that one or more of these things constitutes happiness. [4] If, then, such is the nature of happiness, its component parts must necessarily be:
noble birth, numerous friends, good friends, wealth, good children, numerous children, a good old age; further, bodily excellences, such as health, beauty, strength, stature, fitness for athletic contests, a good reputation, honor, good luck, virtue. For a man would be entirely independent, provided he possessed all internal and external goods; for there are no others. Internal goods are those of mind and body; external goods are noble birth, friends, wealth, honor. To these we think should be added certain capacities and good luck; for on these conditions life will be perfectly secure. Let us now in the same way define each of these in detail.

[5] Noble birth, in the case of a nation or State, means that its members or inhabitants are sprung from the soil, or of long standing; that its first members were famous as leaders, and that many of their descendants have been famous for qualities that are highly esteemed. In the case of private individuals, noble birth is derived from either the father's or the mother's side, and on both sides there must be legitimacy; and, as in the case of a State, it means that its founders were distinguished for virtue, or wealth, or any other of the things that men honor, and that a number of famous persons, both men and women, young and old, belong to the family.

[6] The blessing of good children and numerous children needs little explanation. For the commonwealth it consists in a large number of good young men, good in bodily excellences, such as stature, beauty, strength, fitness for athletic contests; the moral excellences

of a young man are self-control and courage. For the individual it consists in a number of good children of his own, both male and female, and such as we have described. Female bodily excellences are beauty and stature, their moral excellences self-control and industrious habits, free from servility. The object of both the individual and of the community should be to secure the existence of each of these qualities in both men and women; for all those States in which the character of women is unsatisfactory, as in <u>Lacedaemon,</u> may be considered only half-happy.

[7] Wealth consists in abundance of money, ownership of land and properties, and further of movables, cattle, and slaves, remarkable for number, size, and beauty, if they are all secure, liberal, and useful. Property that is productive is more useful, but that which has enjoyment for its object is more liberal. By productive I mean that which is a source of income, by enjoyable that which offers no advantage beyond the use of it—at least, none worth mentioning. Security may be defined
as possession of property in such places and on such conditions that the use of it is in our own hands; and ownership as the right of alienation or not, by which I mean giving the property away or selling it. In a word, being wealthy consists rather in use than in possession; for the actualization and use of such things is wealth.

[8] A good reputation consists in being considered a man of worth by all, or in possessing something of such a nature that all or most men, or the good, or the men of practical wisdom desire it.

[9] Honor is a token of a reputation for doing good; and those who have already done good are justly and above all honored, not but that he who is capable of doing good is also honored. Doing good relates either to personal security and all the causes of existence; or to wealth; or to any other good things which are not easy to acquire, either in any conditions, or at such a place, or at such a time; for many obtain honor for things that appear trifling, but this depends upon place and time. The components of honor are sacrifices, memorials in verse and prose, privileges, grants of land, front seats, public burial, State maintenance, and among the barbarians, prostration and giving place, and all gifts which are highly prized in each country. For a gift is at once a giving of a possession and a token of honor; wherefore gifts are desired by the ambitious and by those who are fond of money,
since they are an acquisition for the latter and an honor for the former; so that they furnish both with what they want.

[10] Bodily excellence is health, and of such a kind that when exercising the body we are free from sickness; for many are healthy in the way Herodicus is said to have been, whom no one would consider happy in the matter of health, because they are obliged to abstain from all or nearly all human enjoyments.

[11] Beauty varies with each age. In a young man, it consists in possessing a body capable of enduring all efforts, either of the racecourse or of bodily strength, while he himself is pleasant to look upon and a sheer delight. This is why the athletes in the pentathlon are most beautiful, because they are naturally adapted for bodily exertion and for swiftness of foot. In a man who has reached his prime, beauty consists in being naturally adapted for the toils of war, in being pleasant to look upon and at the same time awe-inspiring. In an old man, beauty consists in being

naturally adapted to contend with unavoidable labors and in not causing annoyance to others, thanks to the absence of the disagreeable accompaniments of old age.

[12] Strength consists in the power of moving another as one wills, for which purpose it is necessary to pull or push, to lift, to squeeze or crush, so that the strong man is strong by virtue of being able to do all or some of these things.

[13] Excellence of stature consists in being superior to most men in height, depth, and breadth, but in such proportion as not to render the movements of the body slower as the result of excess.

[14] Bodily excellence in athletics consists in size, strength, and swiftness of foot; for to be swift is to be strong. For one who is able to throw his legs about in a certain way, to move them rapidly and with long strides, makes a good runner; one who can hug and grapple, a good wrestler; one who can thrust away by a blow of the fist, a good boxer; one who excels in boxing and wrestling is fit for the pancratium, he who excels in all for the pentathlon.

[15] A happy old age is one that comes slowly with freedom from pain; for neither one who rapidly grows old nor one who grows old insensibly but with pain enjoys a happy old age. This also depends upon bodily excellences and good fortune; for unless a man is free from illness and is strong, he will never be free from suffering, nor will he live long and painlessly without good fortune. Apart from health and strength, however, there is a power of vitality in certain cases; for many live long who are not endowed with bodily excellences. But a minute examination of such questions is needless for the present purpose.

[16] The meaning of numerous and worthy friends is easy to understand from the definition of a friend. A friend is one who exerts himself to do for the sake of another what he thinks is advantageous to him. A man to whom many persons are so disposed, has many friends; if they are virtuous, he has worthy friends.

[17] Good fortune consists in the acquisition or possession
of either all, or the most, or the most important of those goods of which fortune is the cause. Now fortune is the cause of some things with which the arts also are concerned, and also of many which have nothing to do with art, for instance, such as are due to nature （though it is possible that the results of fortune may be contrary to nature） ; for art is a cause of health, but nature of beauty and stature. Speaking generally, the goods which come from fortune are such as excite envy. Fortune is also a cause of those goods which are beyond calculation; for instance, a man's brothers are all ugly, while he is handsome; they did not see the treasure, while he found it; the arrow hit one who stood by and not the man aimed at; or, one who frequented a certain place was the only one who did not go there on a certain occasion, while those who went there then for the first time met their death. All such instances appear to be examples of good fortune.

[18] The definition of virtue, with which the topic of praise is most closely connected, must be left until we come to treat of the latter.

Part 6

6. It is evident, then, what things, likely to happen or already existing, the orator should aim at, when exhorting, and what when dissuading; for they are opposites. But since the aim before the deliberative orator is that which is expedient, and men deliberate, not about the end, but about the means to the end, which are the things which are expedient in regard to our actions; and since, further, the expedient is good, we must first grasp the elementary notions of good and expedient in general.

[2] Let us assume good to be whatever is desirable for its own sake, or for the sake of which we choose something else; that which is the aim of all things, or of all things that possess sensation or reason; or would be, if they could acquire the latter. Whatever reason might assign to each and whatever reason does assign to each in individual cases, that is good for each; and that whose presence makes a man fit and also independent; and independence in general; and that which produces or preserves such things, or on which such things follow, or all that is likely to prevent or destroy their opposites.

[3] Now things follow in two ways—simultaneously or subsequently; for instance, knowledge is subsequent to learning, but life is simultaneous with health. Things which produce act in three ways; thus, healthiness produces health; and so does food; and exercise as a rule. [4] This being laid down, it necessarily follows that the acquisition of good things and the loss of evil things are both good; for it follows simultaneously on the latter that we are rid of that which is bad, and subsequently on the former that we obtain possession of that which is good. [5] The same applies to the acquisition of a greater in place of a less good, and a less in place of a greater evil; for in proportion as the greater exceeds the less, there is an acquisition of the one and a loss of the other. [6] The virtues also must be a good thing; for those who possess them are in a sound condition, and they are also productive of good things and practical. However, we must speak separately concerning each—what it is, and of what kind. [7] Pleasure also must be a good; for all living creatures naturally desire it. Hence it follows that both agreeable and beautiful things must be good; for the former produce pleasure, while among beautiful things some are pleasant and others are desirable in themselves.

[8] To enumerate them one by one, the following things must necessarily be good. Happiness, since it is desirable in itself and self-sufficient, and to obtain it we choose a number of things. [9] Justice, courage, self-control, magnanimity, magnificence, and all other similar states of mind, for they are virtues of the soul. [10] Health, beauty, and the like, for they are virtues of the body and produce many advantages; for instance, health is productive of pleasure and of life, wherefore it is thought to be best of all, because it is the cause of two things which the majority of men prize most highly. [11] Wealth, since it is the excellence of acquisition and productive of many things.
[12] A friend and friendship, since a friend is desirable in himself and produces many advantages. [13] Honor and good repute, since they are agreeable and produce many advantages, and are generally accompanied by the possession of those things for which men are honored.
[14] Eloquence and capacity for action; for all such faculties are productive of many advantages.
[15] Further, natural cleverness, good memory, readiness to learn, quick-wittedness, and all similar qualities; for these faculties are productive of advantages. The same applies to all the

sciences, arts, and even life, for even though no other good should result from it, [16] it is desirable in itself. Lastly, justice, since it is expedient in general for the common weal.

[17] These are nearly all the things generally recognized as good; [18] in the case of doubtful goods, the arguments in their favor are drawn from the following. That is good the opposite of which is evil, [19] or the opposite of which is advantageous to our enemies; for instance, if it is specially advantageous to our enemies that we should be cowards, it is clear that courage is specially advantageous to the citizens. [20] And, speaking generally, the opposite of what our enemies desire or of that in which they rejoice, appears to be advantageous; wherefore it was well said: " Of a truth Priam would exult.

" This is not always the case, but only as a general rule, for there is nothing to prevent one and the same thing being sometimes advantageous to two opposite parties; hence it is said that misfortune brings men together, when a common danger threatens them.

[21] That which is not in excess is good, whereas that which is greater than it should be, is bad. [22] And that which has cost much labor and expense, for it at once is seen to be an apparent good, and such a thing is regarded as an end, and an end of many efforts; now, an end is a good. Wherefore it was said: " And they would [leave Argive Helen for Priam and the Trojans] to boast of,

" and, " It is disgraceful to tarry long,

" and the proverb, "[to break] the pitcher at the door."

[23] And that which many aim at and which is seen to be competed for by many; for that which all aim at was recognized as a good, and the majority may almost stand for "all." [24] And that which is the object of praise, for no one praises that which is not good. And that which is praised by enemies; for if even those who are injured by it acknowledge its goodness, this amounts to a universal recognition of it; for it is because of its goodness being evident that they acknowledge it, just as those whom their enemies praise are worthless. Wherefore the Corinthians imagined themselves insulted by Simonides, when he wrote, " Ilium does not blame the Corinthians.

" [25] And that which one of the practically wise or good, man or woman, has chosen before others, as Athene chose Odysseus, Theseus Helen, the goddesses Alexander Paris, and Homer Achilles.

[26] And, generally speaking, all that is deliberately chosen is good.
Now, men deliberately choose to do the things just mentioned, and those which are harmful to their enemies, and advantageous to their friends, and things which are possible. [27] The last are of two kinds: things which might happen, and things which easily happen; by the latter are meant things that happen without labor or in a short time, for difficulty is defined by labor or length of time. And anything that happens as men wish is good; and what they wish is either what is not evil at all or is less an evil than a good, which will be the case for instance, whenever the penalty attached to it is unnoticed or light. [28] And things that are peculiar to them, or which no one else possesses, or which are out of the common; for thus the honor is greater. And things which

are appropriate to them; such are all things befitting them in respect of birth and power. And things which they think they lack, however unimportant; for none the less they deliberately choose to acquire them. [29] And things which are easy of accomplishment, for being easy they are possible; such things are those in which all, or most men, or those who are equals or inferiors have been successful. And things whereby they will gratify friends or incur the hatred of enemies. And all things that those whom they admire deliberately choose to do. And those things in regard to which they are clever naturally or by experience; for they hope to be more easily successful in them. And things which no worthless man would approve, for that makes them the more commendable. And things which they happen to desire, for such things seem not only agreeable, but also better. [30] Lastly, and above all, each man thinks those things good which are the object of his special desire,

as victory of the man who desires victory, honor of the ambitious man, money of the avaricious, and so in other instances. These then are the materials from which we must draw our arguments in reference to good and the expedient.

Part 7

7. But since men often agree that both of two things are useful, but dispute which is the more so, we must next speak of the greater good and the more expedient. [2] Let one thing, then, be said to exceed another, when it is as great and something more—and to be exceeded when it is contained in the other. "Greater" and "more" always imply a relation with less; "great" and "small," "much" and "little" with the general size of things; the "great" is that which exceeds, and that which falls short of it is "small"; and similarly "much" and "little." [3] Since, besides, we call good that which is desirable for its own sake and not for anything else, and that which all things aim at and which they would choose if they possessed reason and practical wisdom; and that which is productive or protective of good, or on which such things follow; and since that for the sake of which anything is done is the end, and the end is that for the sake of which everything else is done, and that is good for each man which relatively to him presents all these conditions, it necessarily follows that a larger number of good things is a greater good than one or a smaller number, if the one or the smaller number is reckoned as one of them;

for it exceeds them and that which is contained is exceeded.

[4] And if that which is greatest in one class surpass that which is greatest in another class, the first class will surpass the second; and whenever one class surpasses another, the greatest of that class will surpass the greatest of the other. For instance, if the biggest man is greater than the biggest woman, men in general will be bigger than women; and if men in general are bigger than women, the biggest man will be bigger than the biggest woman; for the superiority of classes and of the greatest things contained in them are proportionate. [5] And when this follows on that, but not that on this [then "that" is the greater good]; for the enjoyment of that which follows is contained in that of the other. Now, things follow simultaneously, or successively, or potentially; thus, life follows simultaneously on health, but not health on life; knowledge follows subsequently on learning [but not learning on knowledge]; and simple theft potentially on sacrilege, for one who commits sacrilege will also steal. [6] And things which exceed the same

thing by a greater amount [than something else] are greater, for they must also exceed the greater. [7] And things which produce a greater good are greater; for this we agreed was the meaning of productive of greater. And similarly, that which is produced by a greater cause; for if that which produces health is more desirable than that which produces pleasure and a greater good,
then health is a greater good than pleasure. [8] And that which is more desirable in itself is superior to that which is not; for example, strength is a greater good than the wholesome, which is not desirable for its own sake, while strength is; and, this we agreed was the meaning of a good. [9] And the end is a greater good than the means; for the latter is desirable for the sake of something else, the former for its own sake; for instance, exercise is only a means for the acquirement of a good constitution. [10] And that which has less need of one or several other things in addition is a greater good, for it is more independent (and "having less need" means needing fewer or easier additions. [11] And when one thing does not exist or cannot be brought into existence without the aid of another, but that other can, then that which needs no aid is more independent, and accordingly is seen to be a greater good.

[12] And if one thing is a first principle, and another not; if one thing is a cause and another not, for the same reason; for without cause or first principle nothing can exist or come into existence. And if there are two first principles or two causes, that which results from the greater is greater; and conversely, when there are two first principles or two causes, that which is the first cause or principle of the greater is greater. [13] It is clear then, from what has been said, that a thing may be greater in two ways; for if it is a first principle but another is not, it will appear to be greater, and if it is not a first principle [but an end], while another is; for the end is greater and not a first principle. Thus, Leodamas, when accusing Callistratus, declared that the man who had given the advice
was more guilty than the one who carried it out; for if he had not suggested it, it could not have been carried out. And conversely, when accusing Chabrias, he declared that the man who had carried out the advice was more guilty than the one who had given it; for it could not have been carried out, had there not been some one to do so, and the reason why people devised plots was that others might carry them out.

[14] And that which is scarcer is a greater good than that which is abundant, as gold than iron, although it is less useful, but the possession of it is more valuable, since it is more difficult of acquisition. From another point of view, that which is abundant is to be preferred to that which is scarce, because the use of it is greater, for "often" exceeds "seldom,"; whence the saying: " Water is best.

" [15] And, speaking generally, that which is more difficult is preferable to that which is easier of attainment, for it is scarcer; but from another point of view that which is easier is preferable to that which is more difficult; for its nature is as we wish. [16] And that, the contrary or the deprivation of which is greater, is the greater good. And virtue is greater than non-virtue, and vice than non-vice; for virtues and vices are ends, the others not. [17] And those things whose works are nobler or more disgraceful are themselves greater; and the works of those things, the vices and virtues of which are greater, will also be greater, since between causes and first principles compared with results there is the same relation as between results compared with causes and first principles. [18] Things, superiority in which is more desirable or nobler, are to be preferred; for instance, sharpness of sight is preferable to keenness of smell for sight is better than smell.

And loving one's friends more than money is nobler, whence it follows that love of friends is nobler than love of money. And, on the other hand, the better and nobler things are, the better and nobler will be their superiority; and similarly, those things, the desire for which is nobler and better, are themselves nobler and better, [19] for greater longings are directed towards greater objects. For the same reason, the better and nobler the object, the better and nobler are the desires.

[20] And when the sciences are nobler and more dignified, the nobler and more dignified are their subjects; for as is the science, so is the truth which is its object, and each science prescribes that which properly belongs to it; and, by analogy, the nobler and more dignified the objects of a science, the nobler and more dignified is the science itself, for the same reasons. [21] And that which men of practical wisdom, either all, or more, or the best of them, would judge, or have judged, to be a greater good, must necessarily be such, either absolutely or in so far as they have judged as men of practical wisdom. The same may be said in regard to everything else; for the nature, quantity, and quality of things are such as would be defined by science and practical wisdom. But our statement only applies to goods; for we defined that as good which everything, if possessed of practical wisdom, would choose; hence it is evident that that is a greater good to which practical wisdom assigns the superiority. [22] So also are those things which better men possess, either absolutely, or in so far as they are better; for instance courage is better than strength. And what the better man would choose, either absolutely or in so far as he is better; thus, it is better to suffer wrong than to commit it, for that is what the juster man would choose. [23] And that which is more agreeable rather than that which is less so; for all things pursue pleasure and desire it for its own sake; and it is by these conditions that the good and the end have been defined. And that is more agreeable which is less subject to pain and is agreeable for a longer time. [24] And that which is nobler than that which is less noble; for the noble is that which is either agreeable or desirable in itself. [25] And all things which we have a greater desire to be instrumental in procuring for ourselves or for our friends are greater goods, and those as to which our desire is least are greater evils. [26] And things that last longer are preferable to those that are of shorter duration, and those that are safer to those that are less so; for time increases the use of the first and the wish that of the second; for whenever we wish, we can make greater use of things that are safe.

[27] And things in all cases follow the relations between coordinates and similar inflections; for instance, if "courageously" is nobler than and preferable to "temperately," then "courage" is preferable to "temperance," and it is better to be "courageous" than "temperate." [28] And that which is chosen by all is better than that which is not; and that which the majority choose than that which the minority choose;

for, as we have said, the good is that which all desire, and consequently a good is greater, the more it is desired. The same applies to goods which are recognized as greater by opponents or enemies, by judges, or by those whom they select; for in the one case it would be, so to say, the verdict of all mankind, in the other that of those who are acknowledged authorities and experts. [29] And sometimes a good is greater in which all participate, for it is a disgrace not to participate in it; sometimes when none or only a few participate in it, for it is scarcer. [30] And things which are more praiseworthy, since they are nobler. And in the same way things which are more highly honored, for honor is a sort of measure of worth; and conversely those things are greater evils, the punishment for which is greater. [31] And those things which are greater than what is acknowledged, or appears, to be great, are greater. And the same whole when divided into parts appears greater, for there appears to be superiority in a greater number of things. Whence the poet says that Meleager was persuaded to rise up and fight by the recital of " All the ills that befall those whose city is taken; the people perish, and fire utterly destroys the city, and strangers carry off the children."

Combination and building up, as employed by Epicharmus, produce the same effect as division, and for the same reason; for combination is an exhibition of great superiority and appears to be the origin and cause of great things. [32] And since that which is harder to obtain and scarcer is greater,
it follows that special occasions, ages, places, times, and powers, produce great effects; for if a man does things beyond his powers, beyond his age, and beyond what his equals could do, if they are done in such a manner, in such a place, and at such a time, they will possess importance in actions that are noble, good, or just, or the opposite. Hence the epigram on the Olympian victor: " Formerly, with a rough basket on my shoulders, I used to carry fish from <u>Argos</u> to <u>Tegea</u>.

" And Iphicrates lauded himself, saying, "Look what I started from!" [33] And that which is natural is a greater good than that which is acquired, because it is harder. Whence the poet says: " Self-taught am I.

" [34] And that which is the greatest part of that which is great is more to be desired; as Pericles said in his Funeral Oration, that the removal of the youth from the city was like the year being robbed of its spring. [35] And those things which are available in greater need, as in old age and illness, are greater goods. And of two things that which is nearer the end proposed is preferable. And that which is useful for the individual is preferable to that which is useful absolutely;[16] that which is possible to that which is impossible; for it is the possible that is useful to us, not the impossible. And those things which are at the end of life; for things near the end are more like ends.

[36] And real things are preferable to those that have reference to public opinion, the latter being defined as those which a man would not choose if they were likely to remain unnoticed by others. It would seem then that it is better to receive than to confer a benefit; for one would choose the former even if it should pass unnoticed, whereas one would not choose to confer a benefit, if it were likely to remain unknown. [37] Those things also are to be preferred, which men would rather possess in reality than in appearance, because they are nearer the truth; wherefore it is commonly said that justice is a thing of little importance, because people prefer to appear just than to be just; and this is not the case, for instance, in regard to health. [38] The same may be said of things that serve several ends; for instance, those that assist us to live, to live well, to enjoy life, and to do noble actions; wherefore health and wealth seem to be the greatest goods, for they include all these advantages. [39] And that which is more free from pain and accompanied by pleasure is a greater good; for there is more than one good, since pleasure and freedom from pain combined are both goods. And of two goods the greater is that which, added to one and the same, makes the whole greater. [40] And those things, the presence of

which does not escape notice, are preferable to those which pass unnoticed, because they appear more real; whence being wealthy would appear to be a greater good than the appearance of it. [41] And that which is held most dear, sometimes alone, sometimes accompanied by other things, is a greater good. Wherefore he who puts out the eye of a one-eyed man and he who puts out one eye of another who has two, does not do equal injury; for in the former case, a man has been deprived of that which he held most dear.

Part 8

8. These are nearly all the topics from which arguments
may be drawn in persuading and dissuading; but the most important and effective of all the means of persuasion and good counsel is to know all the forms of government and to distinguish the manners and customs, institutions, and interests of each; [2] for all men are guided by considerations of expediency, and that which preserves the State is expedient. Further, the declaration of the authority is authoritative, and the different kinds of authority are distinguished according to forms of government; in fact, there are as many authorities as there are forms of government.

[3] Now, there are four kinds of government, democracy, oligarchy, aristocracy, monarchy, so that the supreme and deciding authority is always a part or the whole of these. [4] Democracy is a form of government in which the offices are distributed by the people among themselves by lot; in an oligarchy, by those who possess a certain property-qualification; in an aristocracy, by those who possess an educational qualification, meaning an education that is laid down by the law. In fact, in an aristocracy, power and office are in the hands of those who have remained faithful to what the law prescribes, and who must of necessity appear best, whence this form of government has taken its name. In a monarchy, as its name indicates, one man alone is supreme over all;
if it is subject to certain regulations, it is called a kingdom; if it is unlimited, a tyranny.

[5] Nor should the end of each form of government be neglected, for men choose the things which have reference to the end. Now, the end of democracy is liberty, of oligarchy wealth, of aristocracy things relating to education and what the law prescribes, of tyranny self-protection. It is clear then that we must distinguish the manners and customs, institutions, and interests of each form of government, since it is in reference to this that men make their choice. [6] But as proofs are established not only by demonstrative, but also by ethical argument—since we have confidence in an orator who exhibits certain qualities, such as goodness, goodwill, or both—it follows that we ought to be acquainted with the characters of each form of government; for, in reference to each, the character most likely to persuade must be that which is characteristic of it. These characters will be understood by the same means; for characters reveal themselves in accordance with moral purpose, and moral purpose has reference to the end.

[7] We have now stated what things, whether future or present, should be the aim of those who recommend a certain course; from what topics they should derive their proofs of expediency; further, the ways and means of being well equipped for dealing with the characters and

institutions
of each form of government, so far as was within the scope of the present occasion; for the
subject has been discussed in detail in the Politics.

Part 9

9. We will next speak of virtue and vice, of the noble and the disgraceful, since they constitute
the aim of one who praises and of one who blames; for, when speaking of these, we shall
incidentally bring to light the means of making us appear of such and such a character, which, as
we have said, is a second method of proof; for it is by the same means that we shall be able to
inspire confidence in ourselves or others in regard to virtue. [2] But since it happens that men,
seriously or not, often praise not only a man or a god but even inanimate things or any ordinary
animal, we ought in the same way to make ourselves familiar with the propositions relating to
these subjects. Let us, then, discuss these matters also, so far as may serve for illustration.

[3] The noble, then, is that which, being desirable in itself is at the same time worthy of praise, or
which, being good, is pleasant because it is good. If this is the noble, then virtue must of
necessity be noble, for, being good, it is worthy of praise. [4] Virtue, it would seem, is a faculty
of providing and preserving good things, a faculty productive of many and great benefits, in fact,
of all things in all cases.
[5] The components of virtue are justice, courage, self-control, magnificence, magnanimity,
liberality, gentleness, practical and speculative wisdom. [6] The greatest virtues are necessarily
those which are most useful to others, if virtue is the faculty of conferring benefits. For this
reason justice and courage are the most esteemed, the latter being useful to others in war, the
former in peace as well. Next is liberality, for the liberal spend freely and do not dispute the
possession of wealth, which is the chief object of other men's desire. [7] Justice is a virtue which
assigns to each man his due in conformity with the law; injustice claims what belongs to others,
in opposition to the law. [8] Courage makes men perform noble acts in the midst of dangers
according to the dictates of the law and in submission to it; the contrary is cowardice. [9] Self-
control is a virtue which disposes men in regard to the pleasures of the body as the law
prescribes; the contrary is licentiousness. [10] Liberality does good in many matters; the contrary
is avarice. [11] Magnanimity is a virtue productive of great benefits; the contrary is little-
mindedness. [12] Magnificence is a virtue which produces greatness in matters of expenditure;
the contraries are little-mindedness
and meanness. [13] Practical wisdom is a virtue of reason, which enables men to come to a wise
decision in regard to good and evil things, which have been mentioned as connected with
happiness.

[14] Concerning virtue and vice in general and their separate parts, enough has been said for the
moment. To discern the rest presents no difficulty; for it is evident that whatever produces virtue,
as it tends to it, must be noble, and so also must be what comes from virtue; for such are its signs
and works. [15] But since the signs of virtue and such things as are the works and sufferings of a
good man are noble, it necessarily follows that all the works and signs of courage and all
courageous acts are also noble. The same may be said of just things and of just actions;   (but not

of what one suffers justly; for in this alone amongst the virtues that which is justly done is not always noble, and a just punishment is more disgraceful than an unjust punishment) . The same applies equally to the other virtues. [16] Those things of which the reward is honor are noble; also those which are done for honor rather than money. Also, those desirable things which a man does not do for his own sake; [17] things which are absolutely good, which a man has done for the sake of his country, while neglecting his own interests; things which are naturally good; and not such as are good for the individual,
since such things are inspired by selfish motives.

[18] And those things are noble which it is possible for a man to possess after death rather than during his lifetime, for the latter involve more selfishness; [19] all acts done for the sake of others, for they are more disinterested; the successes gained, not for oneself but for others; and for one's benefactors, for that is justice; in a word, all acts of kinds, for they are disinterested. [20] And the contrary of those things of which we are ashamed; for we are ashamed of what is disgraceful, in words, acts, or intention; as, for instance, when Alcaeus said: " I would fain say something, but shame holds me back,

" Sappho rejoined: " Hadst thou desired what was good or noble, and had not thy tongue stirred up some evil to utter it, shame would not have filled thine eyes; but thou would'st have spoken of what is right.

"

[21] Those things also are noble for which men anxiously strive, but without fear; for men are thus affected about goods which lead to good repute. [22] Virtues and actions are nobler, when they proceed from those who are naturally worthier, for instance, from a man rather than from a woman. [23] It is the same with those which are the cause of enjoyment to others rather than to ourselves; this is why justice and that which is just are noble.
[24] To take vengeance on one's enemies is nobler than to come to terms with them; for to retaliate is just, and that which is just is noble; and further, a courageous man ought not to allow himself to be beaten. [25] Victory and honor also are noble; for both are desirable even when they are fruitless, and are manifestations of superior virtue. And things worthy of remembrance, which are the more honorable the longer their memory lasts; those which follow us after death; those which are accompanied by honor; and those which are out of the common. Those which are only possessed by a single individual, because they are more worthy of remembrance. [26] And possessions which bring no profit; for they are more gentlemanly. Customs that are peculiar to individual peoples and all the tokens of what is esteemed among them are noble; for instance, in Lacedaemon it is noble to wear one's hair long, for it is the mark of a gentleman, the performance of any servile task being difficult for one whose hair is long. [27] And not carrying on any vulgar profession is noble, for a gentleman does not live in dependence on others.

[28] We must also assume, for the purpose of praise or blame, that qualities which closely resemble the real qualities are identical with them; for instance, that the cautious man is cold and designing, the simpleton good-natured, and the emotionless gentle. [29] And in each case we must adopt a term from qualities closely connected, always in the more favorable sense; for instance, the choleric and passionate man may be spoken of as frank and open, the arrogant as

magnificent and dignified;

those in excess as possessing the corresponding virtue, the fool-hardy as courageous, the recklessly extravagant as liberal. For most people will think so, and at the same time a fallacious argument may be drawn from the motive; for if a man risks his life when there is no necessity, much more will he be thought likely to do so when it is honorable; and if he is lavish to all comers, the more so will he be to his friends; for the height of virtue is to do good to all. [30] We ought also to consider in whose presence we praise, for, as Socrates said, it is not difficult to praise Athenians among Athenians. We ought also to speak of what is esteemed among the particular audience, Scythians, Lacedaemonians, or philosophers, as actually existing there. And, generally speaking, that which is esteemed should be classed as noble, since there seems to be a close resemblance between the two. [31] Again, all such actions as are in accord with what is fitting are noble; if, for instance, they are worthy of a man's ancestors or of his own previous achievements; for to obtain additional honor is noble and conduces to happiness. Also, if the tendency of what is done is better and nobler, and goes beyond what is to be expected; for instance, if a man is moderate in good fortune and stout-hearted in adversity, or if, when he becomes greater, he is better and more forgiving. Such was the phrase of Iphicrates, "Look what I started from !" and of the Olympian victor: " Formerly, with a rough basket on my shoulders, I used to carry fish from Argos to Tegea.

[32] Since praise is founded on actions, and acting according to moral purpose is characteristic of the worthy man, we must endeavor to show that a man is acting in that manner, and it is useful that it should appear that he has done so on several occasions. For this reason also one must assume that accidents and strokes of good fortune are due to moral purpose; for if a number of similar examples can be adduced, they will be thought to be signs of virtue and moral purpose.

[33] Now praise is language that sets forth greatness of virtue; hence it is necessary to show that a man's actions are virtuous. But encomium deals with achievements—all attendant circumstances, such as noble birth and education, merely conduce to persuasion; for it is probable that virtuous parents will have virtuous offspring and that a man will turn out as he has been brought up. Hence we pronounce an encomium upon those who have achieved something. Achievements, in fact, are signs of moral habit; for we should praise even a man who had not achieved anything, if we felt confident that he was likely to do so. [34] Blessing and felicitation are identical with each other, but are not the same as praise and encomium, which, as virtue is contained in happiness, are contained in felicitation.

[35] Praise and counsels have a common aspect; for what you might suggest in counseling becomes encomium by a change in the phrase.

[36] Accordingly, when we know what we ought to do and the qualities we ought to possess, we ought to make a change in the phrase and turn it, employing this knowledge as a suggestion. For instance, the statement that "one ought not to pride oneself on goods which are due to fortune, but on those which are due to oneself alone," when expressed in this way, has the force of a suggestion; but expressed thus, "he was proud, not of goods which were due to fortune, but of those which were due to himself alone," it becomes praise. Accordingly, if you desire to praise, look what you would suggest; if you desire to suggest, look what you would praise. [37] The form of the expression will necessarily be opposite, when the prohibitive has been changed into

the non-prohibitive.

[38] We must also employ many of the means of amplification; for instance, if a man has done anything alone, or first, or with a few, or has been chiefly responsible for it; all these circumstances render an action noble. Similarly, topics derived from times and seasons, that is to say, if our expectation is surpassed. Also, if a man has often been successful in the same thing; for this is of importance and would appear to be due to the man himself, and not to be the result of chance. And if it is for his sake that distinctions which are an encouragement or honor have been invented and established; and if he was the first on whom an encomium was pronounced, as Hippolochus, or to whom a statue was set up in the market-place, as to Harmodius and Aristogiton. And similarly in opposite cases. If he does not furnish you with enough material in himself,
you must compare him with others, as Isocrates used to do, because of his inexperience of forensic speaking. And you must compare him with illustrious personages, for it affords ground for amplification and is noble, if he can be proved better than men of worth. [39] Amplification is with good reason ranked as one of the forms of praise, since it consists in superiority, and superiority is one of the things that are noble. That is why, if you cannot compare him with illustrious personages, you must compare him with ordinary persons, since superiority is thought to indicate virtue. [40] Speaking generally, of the topics common to all rhetorical arguments, amplification is most suitable for epideictic speakers, whose subject is actions which are not disputed, so that all that remains to be done is to attribute beauty and importance to them. Examples are most suitable for deliberative speakers, for it is by examination of the past that we divine and judge the future. Enthymemes are most suitable for forensic speakers, because the past, by reason of its obscurity, above all lends itself to the investigation of causes and to demonstrative proof. [41] Such are nearly all the materials of praise or blame, the things which those who praise or blame should keep in view, and the sources of encomia and invective; for when these are known their contraries are obvious, since blame is derived from the contrary things.

Part 10

10. We have next to speak of the number and quality of the propositions of which those syllogisms are constructed which have for their object accusation and defence. [2] Three things have to be considered; first, the nature and the number of the motives which lead men to act unjustly; secondly, what is the state of mind of those who so act; thirdly, the character and dispositions of those who are exposed to injustice. [3] We will discuss these questions in order, after we have first defined acting unjustly.

Let injustice, then, be defined as voluntarily causing injury contrary to the law. Now, the law is particular or general. By particular, I mean the written law in accordance with which a state is administered; by general, the unwritten regulations which appear to be universally recognized. Men act voluntarily when they know what they do, and do not act under compulsion. What is done voluntarily is not always done with premeditation; but what is done with premeditation is always known to the agent, for no one is ignorant of what he does with a purpose. [4] The motives which lead men to do injury and commit wrong actions are depravity and incontinence. For if men have one or more vices, it is in that which makes him vicious that he shows himself unjust; for example, the illiberal in regard to money, the licentious in regard to bodily pleasures, the effeminate in regard to what makes for ease, the coward in regard to dangers, for fright makes him desert his comrades in peril;

the ambitious in his desire for honor, the irascible owing to anger, one who is eager to conquer in his desire for victory, the rancorous in his desire for vengeance; the foolish man from having mistaken ideas of right and wrong, the shameless from his contempt for the opinion of others. Similarly, each of the rest of mankind is unjust in regard to his special weakness.

[5] This will be perfectly clear, partly from what has already been said about the virtues, and partly from what will be said about the emotions. It remains to state the motives and character of those who do wrong and of those who suffer from it. [6] First, then, let us decide what those who set about doing wrong long for or avoid; for it is evident that the accuser must examine the number and nature of the motives which are to be found in his opponent; the defendant, which of them are not to be found in him. [7] Now, all human actions are either the result of man's efforts or not. Of the latter some are due to chance, others to necessity. Of those due to necessity, some are to be attributed to compulsion, others to nature, so that the things which men do not do of themselves are all the result of chance, nature, or compulsion. As for those which they do of themselves and of which they are the cause,

some are the result of habit, others of longing, and of the latter some are due to rational, others to irrational longing. [8] Now wish is a [rational] longing for good, for no one wishes for anything unless he thinks it is good; irrational longings are anger and desire. Thus all the actions of men must necessarily be referred to seven causes: chance, nature, compulsion, habit, reason, anger, and desire.

[9] But it is superfluous to establish further distinctions of men's acts based upon age, moral habits, or anything else. For if the young happen to be irascible, or passionately desire anything, it is not because of their youth that they act accordingly, but because of anger and desire. Nor is it because of wealth or poverty; but the poor happen to desire wealth because of their lack of it, and the rich desire unnecessary pleasures because they are able to procure them. Yet in their case too it will not be wealth or poverty, but desire, that will be the mainspring of their action. Similarly, the just and the unjust, and all the others who are said to act in accordance with their moral habits, will act from the same causes, either from reason or emotion, but some from good characters and emotions, and others from the opposite. [10] Not but that it does happen that such and such moral habits are followed by such and such consequences; for it may be that from the outset the fact of being temperate produces in the temperate man good opinions and desires in the matter of pleasant things, in the intemperate man the contrary. [11] Therefore we must leave these distinctions on one side, but we must examine what are the usual consequences of certain conditions. For, if a man is fair or dark, tall or short, there is no rule that any such consequences should follow, but if he is young or old, just or unjust, it does make a difference. In a word, it will be necessary to take account of all the circumstances that make men's characters different; for instance, if a man fancies himself rich or poor, fortunate or unfortunate, it will make a difference. We will, however, discuss this later; let us now speak of what remains to be said here.

[12] Things which are the result of chance are all those of which the cause is indefinite, those which happen without any end in view, and that neither always, nor generally, nor regularly. The definition of chance will make this clear. [13] Things which are the result of nature are all those of which the cause is in themselves and regular;

for they turn out always, or generally, in the same way. As for those which happen contrary to nature there is no need to investigate minutely whether their occurrence is due to a certain force of nature or some other cause [14] (it would seem, however, that such cases also are due to chance). Those things are the result of compulsion which are done by the agents themselves in opposition to their desire or calculation. [15] Things are the result of habit, when they are done because they have often been done. [16] Things are the result of calculation which are done because, of the goods already mentioned, they appear to be expedient either as an end or means to an end, provided they are done by reason of their being expedient; for even the intemperate do certain things that are expedient, for the sake, not of expediency, but of pleasure. Passion and anger are the causes of acts of revenge. [17] But there is a difference between revenge and punishment; the latter is inflicted in the interest of the sufferer, the former in the interest of him who inflicts it, that he may obtain satisfaction. [18] We will define anger when we come to speak of the emotions. Desire is the cause of things being done that are apparently pleasant. The things which are familiar and to which we have become accustomed are among pleasant things; for men do with pleasure many things which are not naturally pleasant, when they have become accustomed to them.

In short, all things that men do of themselves either are, or seem,
good or pleasant; and since men do voluntarily what they do of themselves, and involuntarily what they do not, it follows that all that men do voluntarily will be either that which is or seems good, or that which is or seems pleasant. For I reckon among good things the removal of that which is evil or seems evil, or the exchange of a greater evil for a less, because these two things are in a way desirable; in like manner, I reckon among pleasant things the removal of that which is or appears painful, and the exchange of a greater pain for a less. We must therefore make ourselves acquainted with the number and quality of expedient and pleasant things. [19] We have already spoken of the expedient when discussing deliberative rhetoric; let us now speak of the pleasant. And we must regard our definitions as sufficient in each case, provided they are neither obscure nor too precise.

1 προαίρεσις (premeditation, deliberate or moral choice) is always voluntary, but all voluntary action is not premeditated; we sometimes act on the spur of the moment. Choice is a voluntary act, the result of deliberate counsel, including the use of reason and knowledge. In **Aristot. Nic. Eth. 11** Aristotle defines προαίρεσις as "a deliberate appetition of (longing for, ὄρεξις) things in our power," as to which we should necessarily be well-informed.

2 Or, "in the matter of ease," taking τὰ ῥάθυμα as = ῥαθυμία.

3 In the cases of the young, the poor, and the rich, their youth etc. are only "accidents," accidental not real causes. Aristotle defines τὸ συμβεβηκός (**Aristot. Met. 4.30**) as "that which is inherent in something, and may be predicated of it as true, but neither necessarily, nor in most cases; for instance, if a man, when digging a hole for a plant, finds a treasure." The color of

a man's eyes is an "inseparable" accident, the fact that a man is a lawyer is a "separable" accident.

4 Book 2.12-18.

5 Book 2.2.

6 Cf. Book 1.6 above.

Part 11

11. Let it be assumed by us that pleasure is a certain movement of the soul, a sudden and perceptible settling down into its natural state, and pain the opposite. [2] If such is the nature of pleasure,
it is evident that that which produces the disposition we have just mentioned is pleasant, and that that which destroys it or produces the contrary settling down is painful. [3] Necessarily,
therefore, it must be generally pleasant to enter into a normal state （especially when what is done in accordance with that state has come into its own again）¹; and the same with habits. For that which has become habitual becomes as it were natural; in fact, habit is something like nature, for the distance between "often" and "always" is not great, and nature belongs to the idea of "always," habit to that of "often." [4] That which is not compulsory is also pleasant, for compulsion is contrary to nature. That is why what is necessary is painful, and it was rightly said, " For every act of necessity is disagreeable.²

" Application, study, and intense effort are also painful, for these involve necessity and compulsion, if they have not become habitual; for then habit makes them pleasant. Things contrary to these are pleasant; wherefore states of ease, idleness, carelessness, amusement, recreation,³ and sleep are among pleasant things, because none of these is in any way compulsory. [5] Everything of which we have in us the desire is pleasant, for desire is a longing for the pleasant.

Now, of desires some are irrational, others rational. I call irrational all those that are not the result of any
assumption.⁴ Such are all those which are called natural; for instance, those which come into existence through the body—such as the desire of food, thirst, hunger, the desire of such and such food in particular; the desires connected with taste, sexual pleasures, in a word, with touch, smell, hearing, and sight. I call those desires rational which are due to our being convinced; for there are many things which we desire to see or acquire when we have heard them spoken of and are convinced that they are pleasant.

[6] And if pleasure consists in the sensation of a certain emotion, and imagination is a weakened sensation, then both the man who remembers and the man who hopes will be attended by an imagination of what he remembers or hopes.⁵ This being so, it is evident that there is pleasure both for those who remember and for those who hope, since there is sensation. [7] Therefore all

pleasant things must either be present in sensation, or past in recollection, or future in hope; for one senses the present, recollects the past, and hopes for the future.

[8] Therefore our recollections are pleasant, not only when they recall things which when present were agreeable, but also some things which were not, if their consequence subsequently proves honorable or good; whence the saying: " Truly it is pleasant to remember toil after one has escaped it,[6]

" and, " When a man has suffered much and accomplished much, he afterwards takes pleasure even in his sorrows when he recalls them.

" [9] The reason of this is that even to be free from evil is pleasant. Things which we hope for are pleasant, when their presence seems likely to afford us great pleasure or advantage, without the accompaniment of pain. In a word, all things that afford pleasure by their presence as a rule also afford pleasure when we hope for or remember them. Wherefore even resentment is pleasant, as Homer said of anger that it is " Far sweeter than dripping honey;

" for no one feels resentment against those whom vengeance clearly cannot overtake, or those who are far more powerful than he is; against such, men feel either no resentment or at any rate less.

[10] Most of our desires are accompanied by a feeling of pleasure, for the recollection of a past or the hope of a future pleasure creates a certain pleasurable enjoyment; thus, those suffering from fever and tormented by thirst enjoy the remembrance of having drunk and the hope that they will drink again. [11] The lovesick always take pleasure in talking, writing, or composing verses about the beloved; for it seems to them that in all this recollection makes the object of their affection perceptible. Love always begins in this manner, when men are happy not only in the presence of the beloved, but also in his absence when they recall him to mind. [12] This is why, even when his absence is painful, there is a certain amount of pleasure even in mourning and lamentation; for the pain is due to his absence, but there is pleasure in remembering and, as it were, seeing him and recalling his actions and personality. Wherefore it was rightly said by the poet; " Thus he spake, and excited in all a desire of weeping.

"

[13] And revenge is pleasant; for if it is painful to be unsuccessful, it is pleasant to succeed. Now, those who are resentful are pained beyond measure when they fail to secure revenge, while the hope of it delights them. [14] Victory is pleasant, not only to those who love to conquer, but to all; for there is produced an idea of superiority, which all with more or less eagerness desire. [15] And since victory is pleasant, competitive and disputatious amusements must be so too, for victories are often gained in them; among these we may include games with knuckle-bones, ball-games, dicing, and draughts. It is the same with serious sports; for some become pleasant when one is familiar with them, while others are so from the outset, such as the chase and every description of outdoor sport; for rivalry implies victory. It follows from this that practice in the law courts and disputation are pleasant to those who are familiar with them and well qualified. [16] Honor and good repute are among the most pleasant things, because every one imagines that he possesses the qualities of a worthy man, and still more when those whom he believes to be

trustworthy say that he does. Such are neighbors rather than those who live at a distance; intimate friends and fellow-citizens rather than those who are unknown; contemporaries rather than those who come later; the sensible rather than the senseless; the many rather than the few; for such persons are more likely to be trustworthy than their opposites. As for those for whom men feel great contempt, such as children and animals, they pay no heed to their respect or esteem, or, if they do, it is not for the sake of their esteem, but for some other reason.

[17] A friend also is among pleasant things, for it is pleasant to love—for no one loves wine unless he finds pleasure in it—just as it is pleasant to be loved; for in this case also a man has an impression that he is really endowed with good qualities, a thing desired by all who perceive it; and to be loved is to be cherished for one's own sake. [18] And it is pleasant to be admired, because of the mere honor. Flattery and the flatterer are pleasant, the latter being a sham admirer and friend. [19] It is pleasant to do the same things often; for that which is familiar is, as we said, pleasant. [20] Change also is pleasant, since change is in the order of nature; for perpetual sameness creates an excess of the normal condition; whence it was said: " Change in all things is sweet.

" This is why what we only see at intervals, whether men or things, is pleasant; for there is a change from the present, and at the same time it is rare. [21] And learning and admiring are as a rule pleasant; for admiring implies the desire to learn, so that what causes admiration is to be desired, and learning implies a return to the normal. [22] It is pleasant to bestow and to receive benefits; the latter is the attainment of what we desire, the former the possession of more than sufficient means, both of them things that men desire. Since it is pleasant to do good, it must also be pleasant for men to set their neighbors on their feet, and to supply their deficiencies. [23] And since learning and admiring are pleasant, all things connected with them must also be pleasant; for instance, a work of imitation, such as painting, sculpture, poetry, and all that is well imitated, even if the object of imitation is not pleasant; for it is not this that causes pleasure or the reverse, but the inference that the imitation and the object imitated are identical, so that the result is that we learn something. [24] The same may be said of sudden changes and narrow escapes from danger; for all these things excite wonder. [25] And since that which is in accordance with nature is pleasant, and things which are akin are akin in accordance with nature, all things akin and like are for the most part pleasant to each other, as man to man; horse to horse, youth to youth. This is the origin of the proverbs: "The old have charms for the old, the young for the young,""Like to like,""Beast knows beast,""Birds of a feather flock together," and all similar sayings.

[26] And since things which are akin and like are always pleasant to one another, and every man in the highest degree feels this in regard to himself, it must needs be that all men are more or less selfish; for it is in himself above all that such conditions are to be found. Since, then, all men are selfish, it follows that all find pleasure in what is their own, such as their works and words. That is why men as a rule are fond of those who flatter and love them, of honor, and of children; for the last are their own work. It is also pleasant to supply what is wanting, [27] for then it becomes our work. And since it is most pleasant to command, it is also pleasant to be regarded as wise for practical wisdom is commanding, and philosophy consists In the knowledge of many things that excite wonder. Further, since men are generally ambitious, it follows that it is also agreeable to find fault with our neighbors. [28] And if a man thinks he

excels in anything, he likes to devote his time to it; as Euripides says: " And allotting the best part of each day to that in which he happens to surpass himself, he presses eagerly towards it.

" [29] Similarly, since amusement, every kind of relaxation, and laughter are pleasant, ridiculous things—men, words, or deeds—must also be pleasant.

The ridiculous has been discussed separately in the Poetics. Let this suffice for things that are pleasant; those that are painful will be obvious from the contraries of these.

Part 12

12. Such are the motives of injustice; let us now state the frame of mind of those who commit it, and who are the sufferers from it. Men do wrong when they think that it can be done and that it can be done by them; when they think that their action will either be undiscovered, or if discovered will remain unpunished; or if it is punished, that the punishment will be less than the profit to themselves or to those for whom they care. [2] As for the kind of things which seem possible or impossible, we will discuss them later, for these topics are common to all kinds of rhetoric. Now men who commit wrong think they are most likely to be able to do so with impunity, if they are eloquent, business-like, experienced in judicial trials, if they have many friends, and if they are wealthy. [3] They think there is the greatest chance of their being able to do so, if they themselves belong to the above classes; if not, if they have friends, servants, or accomplices who do; for thanks to these qualities they are able to commit wrong and to escape discovery and punishment. [4] Similarly, if they are friends of those who are being wronged, or of the judges; for friends are not on their guard against being wronged and, besides, they prefer reconciliation

to taking proceedings; and judges favor those whom they are fond of, and either let them off altogether or inflict a small penalty.

[5] Those are likely to remain undetected whose qualities are out of keeping with the charges, for instance, if a man wanting in physical strength were accused of assault and battery, or a poor and an ugly man of adultery. Also, if the acts are done quite openly and in sight of all; for they are not guarded against, because no one would think them possible. [6] Also, if they are so great and of such a nature that no one would even be likely to attempt them, for these also are not guarded against; for all guard against ordinary ailments and wrongs, but no one takes precautions against those ailments from which no one has ever yet suffered. [7] And those who have either no enemy at all or many; the former hope to escape notice because they are not watched, the latter do escape because they would not be thought likely to attack those who are on their guard and because they can defend themselves by the plea that they would never have attempted it. [8] And, those who have ways or places of concealment for stolen property, or abundant opportunities of disposing of it. And those who, even if they do not remain undetected, can get the trial set aside or put off, or corrupt the judges. And those who, if a fine be imposed, can get payment in full set aside or put off for a long time, or those who, owing to poverty, have nothing to lose. [9] And in cases where the profit is certain, large, or immediate, while the punishment is small, uncertain, or remote.

And where there can be no punishment equal to the advantages, as seems to be the case in a tyranny. [10] And when the unjust acts are real gains and the only punishment is disgrace; and when, on the contrary, the unjust acts tend to our credit, for instance, if one avenges father or mother, as was the case with Zeno, while the punishment only involves loss of money, exile, or something of the kind. For men do wrong from both these motives and in both these conditions of mind; but the persons are not the same, and their characters are exactly opposite. [11] And those who have often been undetected or have escaped punishment; and those who have often been unsuccessful; for in such cases, as in actual warfare, there are always men ready to return to the fight. [12] And all who hope for pleasure and profit at once, while the pain and the loss come later; such are the intemperate, intemperance being concerned with all things that men long for. [13] And when, on the contrary, the pain or the loss is immediate, while the pleasure and the profit are later and more lasting; for temperate and wiser men pursue such aims. [14] And those who may possibly be thought to have acted by chance or from necessity, from some natural impulse or from habit, in a word, to have committed an error rather than a crime. [15] And those who hope to obtain indulgence; and all those who are in need, which is of two kinds; for men either need what is necessary, as the poor, or what is superfluous, as the wealthy. [16] And those who are highly esteemed or held in great contempt; the former will not be suspected, the latter no more than they are already.

[17] In such a frame of mind men attempt to do wrong, and the objects of their wrongdoing are men and circumstances of the following kind. Those who possess what they themselves lack, things either necessary, or superfluous, or enjoyable; [18] both those who are far off and those who are near, for in the one case the gain is speedy, in the other reprisals are slow, as if, for instance, Greeks were to plunder Carthaginians. [19] And those who never take precautions and are never on their guard, but are confiding; for all these are easily taken unawares. And those who are indolent; for it requires a man who takes pains to prosecute. And those who are bashful; for they are not likely to fight about money. [20] And those who have often been wronged but have not prosecuted, being, as the proverb says, "Mysian booty." [21] And those who have never, or those who have often, suffered wrong; for both are off their guard, the one because they have never yet been attacked, the others because they do not expect to be attacked again. [22] And those who have been slandered, or are easy to slander; for such men neither care to go to law, for fear of the judges, nor, if they do, can they convince them; to this class belong those who are exposed to hatred or envy.
[23] And those against whom the wrongdoer can pretend that either their ancestors, or themselves, or their friends, have either committed, or intended to commit, wrong either against himself, or his ancestors, or those for whom he has great regard; for, as the proverb says, "evil-doing only needs an excuse." [24] And both enemies and friends; for it is easy to injure the latter, and pleasant to injure the former. And those who are friendless. And those who are unskilled in speech or action; for either they make no attempt to prosecute, or come to terms, or accomplish nothing. [25] And those to whom it is no advantage to waste time waiting for the verdict or damages, such as strangers or husbandmen; for they are ready to compromise on easy terms and to drop proceedings. [26] And those who have committed numerous wrongs, or such as those from which they themselves are suffering; for it seems almost an act of justice that a man should suffer a wrong such as he had been accustomed to make others suffer; if, for instance, one were to assault a man who was in the habit of outraging others. [27] And those who have already injured us, or intended, or intend, or are about to do so; for in such a case vengeance is both pleasant and honorable, and seems to be almost an act of justice. [28] And those whom we

wrong in order to ingratiate ourselves with our friends, or persons whom we admire or love, or our masters, in a word, those by whom our life is ruled. [29] And those in reference to whom there is a chance of obtaining merciful consideration. And those against whom we have a complaint, or with whom we have had a previous difference, as Callippus acted in the matter of Dion; for in such cases it seems almost an act of justice. [30] And those who are going to be attacked by others, if we do not attack first, since it is no longer possible to deliberate; thus, Aenesidemus is said to have sent the prize in the game of cottabus to Gelon, who, having reduced a town to slavery, had anticipated him by doing what he had intended to do himself. [31] And those to whom, after having injured them, we shall be enabled to do many acts of justice, in the idea that it will be easy to repair the wrong; as Jason the Thessalian said one should sometimes commit injustice, in order to be able also to do justice often.

[32] Men are ready to commit wrongs which all or many are in the habit of committing, for they hope to be pardoned for their offences. [33] They steal objects that are easy to conceal; such are things that are quickly consumed, as eatables; things which can easily be changed in form or color or composition; [34] things for which there are many convenient hiding-places, such as those that are easy to carry or stow away in a corner; [35] those of which a thief already possesses a considerable number exactly similar or hard to distinguish. Or they commit wrongs which the victims are ashamed to disclose, such as outrages upon the women of their family, upon themselves, or upon their children. And all those wrongs in regard to which appeal to the law would create the appearance of litigiousness; such are wrongs which are unimportant or venial. These are nearly all the dispositions which induce men to commit wrong, the nature and motive of the wrongs, and the kind of persons who are the victims of wrong.

Part 13

13. Let us now classify just and unjust actions generally, starting from what follows. Justice and injustice have been defined in reference to laws and persons in two ways. [2] Now there are two kinds of laws, particular and general. By particular laws I mean those established by each people in reference to themselves, which again are divided into written and unwritten; by general laws I mean those based upon nature. In fact, there is a general idea of just and unjust in accordance with nature, as all men in a manner divine, even if there is neither communication nor agreement between them. This is what Antigone in Sophocles evidently means, when she declares that it is just, though forbidden, to bury Polynices, as being naturally just: " For neither to-day nor yesterday, but from all eternity, these statutes live and no man knoweth whence they came.

" And as Empedocles says in regard to not killing that which has life, for this is not right for some and wrong for others, " But a universal precept, which extends without a break throughout the wide-ruling sky and the boundless earth.

" Alcidamas also speaks of this precept in his Messeniacus. . . . [3] And in relation to persons, there is a twofold division of law; for what one ought to do or ought not to do is concerned with the community generally, or one of its members.

Therefore there are two kinds of just and unjust acts, since they can be committed against a definite individual or against the community; he who commits adultery or an assault is guilty of wrong against a definite individual, he who refuses to serve in the army of wrong against the State. [4] All kinds of wrong acts having been thus distinguished, some of which affect the State, others one or several individuals, let us repeat the definition of being wronged, and then go on to the rest. [5] Being wronged is to suffer injustice at the hands of one who voluntarily inflicts it, for it has been established that injustice is a voluntary act. [6] And since the man who suffers injustice necessarily sustains injury and that against his will, it is evident from what has been said in what the injuries consist; for things good and bad have already been distinguished in themselves, and it has been said that voluntary acts are all such as are committed with knowledge of the case. [7] Hence it necessarily follows that all accusations concern the State or the individual, the accused having acted either ignorantly and against his will, or voluntarily and with knowledge, and in the latter case with malice aforethought or from passion. [8] We will speak of anger when we come to treat of the passions, and we have already stated in what circumstances and with what dispositions men act with deliberate purpose.

[9] But since a man, while admitting the fact, often denies the description of the charge or the point on which it turns—for instance, admits that he took something, but did not steal it; that he was the first to strike, but committed no outrage; that he had relations, but did not commit adultery, with a woman; or that he stole something but was not guilty of sacrilege, since the object in question was not consecrated; or that he trespassed, but not on public land; or that he held converse with the enemy, but was not guilty of treason—for this reason it will be necessary that a definition should be given of theft, outrage, or adultery, in order that, if we desire to prove that an offence has or has not been committed, we may be able to put the case in a true light. [10] In all such instances the question at issue is to know whether the supposed offender is a wrongdoer and a worthless person, or not; for vice and wrongdoing consist in the moral purpose, and such terms as outrage and theft further indicate purpose; for if a man has struck, it does not in all cases follow that he has committed an outrage, but only if he has struck with a certain object, for instance, to bring disrepute upon the other or to please himself. Again, if a man has taken something by stealth, it is by no means certain that he has committed theft, but only if he has taken it to injure another or to get something for himself. It is the same in all other cases as in these.

[11] We have said that there are two kinds of just and unjust actions (for some are written, but others are unwritten) and have spoken of those concerning which the laws are explicit; of those that are unwritten there are two kinds. [12] One kind arises from an excess of virtue or vice, which is followed by praise or blame, honor or dishonor, and rewards; for instance, to be grateful to a benefactor, to render good for good, to help one's friends, and the like; the other kind contains what is omitted in the special written law. [13] For that which is equitable seems to be just, and equity is justice that goes beyond the written law. These omissions are sometimes involuntary, sometimes voluntary, on the part of the legislators; involuntary when it may have escaped their notice, voluntary when, being unable to define for all cases, they are obliged to make a universal statement, which is not applicable to all, but only to most, cases; and whenever it is difficult to give a definition owing to the infinite number of cases, as, for instance, the size and kind of an iron instrument used in wounding; for life would not be long enough to reckon all the possibilities. [14] If then no exact definition is possible, but legislation is necessary, one must have recourse to general terms; so that, if a man wearing a ring lifts up his hand to strike or

actually strikes, according to the written law he is guilty of wrongdoing, but in reality he is not; and this is a case for equity.

[15] If then our definition of equity is correct, it is easy to see what things and persons are equitable or not. [16] Actions which should be leniently treated are cases for equity; errors, wrong acts, and misfortunes, must not be thought deserving of the same penalty. Misfortunes are all such things as are unexpected and not vicious; errors are not unexpected, but are not vicious; wrong acts are such as might be expected and vicious, for acts committed through desire arise from vice. [17] And it is equitable to pardon human weaknesses, and to look, not to the law but to the legislator; not to the letter of the law but to the intention of the legislator; not to the action itself, but to the moral purpose; [18] not to the part, but to the whole; not to what a man is now, but to what he has been, always or generally; to remember good rather than ill treatment, and benefits received rather than those conferred; to bear injury with patience; to be willing to appeal to the judgement of reason rather than to violence; [19] to prefer
arbitration to the law court, for the arbitrator keeps equity in view, whereas the dicast looks only to the law, and the reason why arbitrators were appointed was that equity might prevail. Let this manner of defining equity suffice.

Part 14

14. Wrong acts are greater in proportion to the injustice from which they spring. For this reason the most trifling are sometimes the greatest, as in the charge brought by Callistratus against Melanopus that he had fraudulently kept back three consecrated half-obols from the temple-builders[2]; whereas, in the case of just actions, it is quite the contrary. The reason is that the greater potentially inheres in the less; for he who has stolen three consecrated half-obols will commit any wrong whatever. Wrong acts are judged greater sometimes in this way, sometimes by the extent of the injury done. [2] A wrong act is greater when there is no adequate punishment for it, but all are insufficient; when there is no remedy, because it is difficult if not impossible to repair it; and when the person injured cannot obtain legal satisfaction, since it is irremediable; for justice and punishment are kinds of remedies. [3] And if the sufferer, having been wronged, has inflicted some terrible injury upon himself, the guilty person deserves greater punishment; wherefore Sophocles, when pleading on behalf of Euctemon, who had committed suicide after the outrage he had suffered,
declared that he would not assess the punishment at less than the victim had assessed it for himself. [4] A wrong act is also greater when it is unprecedented, or the first of its kind, or when committed with the aid of few accomplices; and when it has been frequently committed; or when because of it new prohibitions and penalties have been sought and found: thus, at Argos the citizen owing to whom a new law has been passed, is punished, as well as those on whose account a new prison had to be built. [5] The crime is greater, the more brutal it is; or when it has been for a long time premeditated; when the recital of it inspires terror rather than pity. Rhetorical tricks of the following kind may be used:—the statement that the accused person has swept away or violated several principles of justice, for example, oaths, pledges of friendship, plighted word, the sanctity of marriage; for this amounts to heaping crime upon crime. [6] Wrong acts are greater when committed in the very place where wrongdoers themselves are

sentenced, as is done by false witnesses; for where would a man not commit wrong, if he does so in a court of justice? They are also greater when accompanied by the greatest disgrace; when committed against one who has been the guilty person's benefactor, for in that case, the wrongdoer is guilty of wrong twice over, in that he not only does wrong, but does not return good for good. [7] So too, again, when a man offends against the unwritten laws of right, for there is greater merit in doing right without being compelled; now the written laws involve compulsion, the unwritten do not. Looked at in another way, wrongdoing is greater, if it violates the written laws; for a man who commits wrongs that alarm him and involve punishment, will be ready to commit wrong

for which he will not be punished. Let this suffice for the treatment of the greater or less degree of wrongdoing.

Part 15

15. Following on what we have just spoken of, we have now briefly to run over what are called the inartificial proofs, for these properly belong to forensic oratory. [2] These proofs are five in number: laws, witnesses, contracts, torture, oaths. [3] Let us first then speak of the laws, and state what use should be made of them when exhorting or dissuading, accusing or defending. [4] For it is evident that, if the written law is counter to our case, we must have recourse to the general law and equity, as more in accordance with justice; [5] and we must argue that, when the dicast takes an oath to decide to the best of his judgement, he means that he will not abide rigorously by the written laws; [6] that equity is ever constant and never changes, even as the general law, which is based on nature, whereas the written laws often vary (this is why Antigone in Sophocles justifies herself for having buried Polynices contrary to the law of Creon, but not contrary to the unwritten law:

" For this law is not of now or yesterday, but is eternal . . . this I was not likely [to infringe through fear of the pride] of any man)

" [7] and further, that justice is real and expedient, but not that which only appears just; nor the written law either, because it does not do the work of the law; that the judge is like an assayer of silver, whose duty is to distinguish spurious from genuine justice; [8] that it is the part of a better man to make use of and abide by the unwritten rather than the written law.[9] Again, it is necessary to see whether the law is contradictory to another approved law or to itself; for instance, one law enacts that all contracts should be binding, while another forbids making contracts contrary to the law. [10] If the meaning of the law is equivocal, we must turn it about, and see in which way it is to be interpreted so as to suit the application of justice or expediency, and have recourse to that. [11] If the conditions which led to the enactment of the law are now obsolete, while the law itself remains, one must endeavor to make this clear and to combat the law by this argument. [12] But if the written law favors our case, we must say that the oath of the dicast "to decide to the best of his judgement" does not justify him in deciding contrary to the law, but is only intended to relieve him from the charge of perjury, if he is ignorant of the meaning of the law; that no one chooses that which is good absolutely, but that which is good for himself;

that there is no difference between not using the laws and their not being enacted; that in the other arts there is no advantage in trying to be wiser than the physician, for an error on his part does not do so much harm as the habit of disobeying the authority; that to seek to be wiser than the laws is just what is forbidden in the most approved laws. Thus much for the laws.

[13] Witnesses are of two kinds, ancient and recent; of the latter some share the risk of the trial, others are outside it. By ancient I mean the poets and men of repute whose judgements are known to all; for instance, the Athenians, in the matter of <u>Salamis</u>, appealed to Homer as a witness, and recently the inhabitants of <u>Tenedos</u> to Periander of <u>Corinth</u> against the Sigeans. Cleophon also made use of the elegiacs of Solon against Critias, to prove that his family had long been notorious for licentiousness, otherwise Solon would never have written: " Bid me the fair-haired Critias listen to his father.

" [14] One should appeal to such witnesses for the past,
but also to interpreters of oracles for the future; thus, for instance, Themistocles interpreted the wooden wall to mean that they must fight at sea. Further, proverbs, as stated, are evidence; for instance, if one man advises another not to make a friend of an old man, he can appeal to the proverb, "Never do good to an old man." And if he advises another to kill the children, after having killed the fathers, he can say, " Foolish is he who, having killed the father, suffers the children to live.

"

[15] By recent witnesses I mean all well-known persons who have given a decision on any point, for their decisions are useful to those who are arguing about similar cases. Thus for instance, Eubulus, when attacking Chares in the law courts, made use of what Plato said against Archibius, namely, "that the open confession of wickedness had increased in the city." [16] And those who share the risk of the trial, if they are thought to be perjurers. Such witnesses only serve to establish whether an act has taken place or not, whether it is or is not the case; but if it is a question of the quality of the act, for instance, whether it is just or unjust, expedient or inexpedient, [17] they are not competent witnesses; but witnesses from a distance are very trustworthy even in regard to this. But ancient witnesses are the most trustworthy of all, for they cannot be corrupted. In regard to the confirmation of evidence, when a man has no witnesses, he can say that the decision should be given in accordance with probabilities, and that this is the meaning of the oath "according to the best of one's judgement"; that probabilities cannot be bribed to deceive, and that they cannot be convicted of bearing false witness. But if a man has witnesses and his adversary has none, he can say that probabilities incur no responsibility, and that there would have been no need of evidence, if an investigation according to the arguments were sufficient. [18] Evidence partly concerns ourselves, partly our adversary, as to the fact itself or moral character; so that it is evident that one never need lack useful evidence. For, if we have no evidence as to the fact itself, neither in confirmation of our own case nor against our opponent, it will always be possible to obtain some evidence as to character that will establish either our own respectability or the worthlessness of our opponent. [19] As for all the other questions relative to a witness, whether he is a friend, an enemy, or neutral, of good or bad or middling reputation, and for all other differences of this kind, we must have recourse to the same topics as those from which we derive our enthymemes.

[20] As for contracts, argument may be used to the extent of magnifying or minimizing their

importance, of proving that they do or do not deserve credit.

If we have them on our side, we must try to prove them worthy of credit and authoritative; but if they are on the side of our opponent, we must do the opposite. [21] In view of rendering them worthy or unworthy of credit, the method of procedure is exactly the same as in the case of witnesses; for contracts are trustworthy according to the character of their signatories or depositaries. When the existence of the contract is admitted, if it is in our favor, we must strengthen it by asserting that the contract is a law, special and partial; and it is not the contracts that make the law authoritative, but it is the laws that give force to legal contracts. And in a general sense the law itself is a kind of contract, so that whoever disobeys or subverts a contract, subverts the laws. [22] Further, most ordinary and all voluntary transactions are carried out according to contract; so that if you destroy the authority of contracts, the mutual intercourse of men is destroyed. All other arguments suitable to the occasion are easy to see. [23] But if the contract is against us and in favor of our opponents, in the first place those arguments are suitable which we should oppose to the law if it were against us; that it would be strange if, while we consider ourselves entitled to refuse to obey ill-made laws, whose authors have erred, we should be obliged to consider ourselves always bound by contracts. [24] Or, that the judge is the dispenser of justice; so that it is not the contents of the contract that he has to consider, but what is juster. [25] Further, that one cannot alter justice either by fraud or compulsion, for it is based upon nature, whereas contracts may be entered into under both conditions. In addition to this, we must examine whether the contract is contrary to any written law of our own or foreign countries, or to any general law, or to other previous or subsequent contracts. For either the latter are valid and the former not, or the former are right and the latter fraudulent; we may put it in whichever way it seems fit. We must also consider the question of expediency—whether the contract is in any way opposed to the interest of the judges. There are a number of other arguments of the same kind, which are equally easy to discern.

[26] Torture is a kind of evidence, which appears trustworthy, because a sort of compulsion is attached to it. Nor is it difficult to see what may be said concerning it, and by what arguments, if it is in our favor, we can exaggerate its importance by asserting that it is the only true kind of evidence;

but if it is against us and in favor of our opponent, we can destroy its value by telling the truth about all kinds of torture generally; for those under compulsion are as likely to give false evidence as true, some being ready to endure everything rather than tell the truth, while others are equally ready to make false charges against others, in the hope of being sooner released from torture. It is also necessary to be able to quote actual examples of the kind with which the judges are acquainted. It may also be said that evidence given under torture is not true; for many thick-witted and thick-skinned persons, and those who are stout-hearted heroically hold out under sufferings, while the cowardly and cautious, before they see the sufferings before them, are bold enough; wherefore evidence from torture may be considered utterly untrustworthy.

[27] As to oaths four divisions may be made; for either we tender an oath and accept it, or we do neither, or one without the other, and in the last case we either tender but do not accept, or accept but do not tender. Besides this, one may consider whether the oath has already been taken by us or by the other party. [28] If you do not tender the oath to the adversary, it is because men readily perjure themselves, and because, after he has taken the oath, he will refuse to repay the money, while, if he does not take the oath, you think that the dicasts will condemn him; and also because

the risk incurred in leaving the decision to the dicasts is preferable, for you have confidence in them, but not in your adversary. [29] If you refuse to take the oath yourself, you may argue that the oath is only taken with a view to money; that, if you had been a scoundrel, you would have taken it at once, for it is better to be a scoundrel for something than for nothing; that, if you take it, you will win your case, if not, you will probably lose it; consequently, your refusal to take it is due to moral excellence, not to fear of committing perjury. And the apophthegm of Xenophanes is apposite— that "it is unfair
for an impious man to challenge a pious one," for it is the same as a strong man challenging a weak one to hit or be hit. [30] If you accept the oath, you may say that you have confidence in yourself, but not in your opponent, and, reversing the apophthegm of Xenophanes, that the only fair way is that the impious man should tender the oath and the pious man take it; and that it would be monstrous to refuse to take the oath yourself, while demanding that the judges should take it before giving their verdict. [31] But if you tender the oath, you may say that it is an act of piety to be willing to leave the matter to the gods; that your opponent has no need to look for other judges, for you allow him to make the decision himself; [32] and that it would be ridiculous that he should be unwilling to take an oath in cases where he demands that the dicasts should take one.

Now, since we have shown how we must deal with each case individually, it is clear how we must deal with them when taken two and two; for instance, if we wish to take the oath but not to tender it, to tender it but not to take it, to accept and tender it, or to do neither the one nor the other.
For such cases, and similarly the arguments, must be a combination of those already mentioned. And if we have already taken an oath which contradicts the present one, we may argue that it is not perjury; for whereas wrongdoing is voluntary, and perjury is wrongdoing, what is done in error or under compulsion is involuntary. [33] Here we must draw the conclusion that perjury consists in the intention, not in what is said. But if the opponent has taken such an oath, we may say that one who does not abide by what be has sworn subverts everything, for this is the reason why the dicasts take an oath before applying the laws; and [we may make this appeal]: "They demand that you abide by your oath as judges, while they themselves do not abide by theirs." Further, we should employ all means of amplification. Let this suffice for the inartificial proofs.

BOOK II

Part 1

We have now considered the materials to be used in supporting or opposing a political measure, in pronouncing eulogies or censures, and for prosecution and defence in the law courts. We have considered the received opinions on which we may best base our arguments so as to convince our hearers-those opinions with which our enthymemes deal, and out of which they are built, in each of the three kinds of oratory, according to what may be called the special needs of each.

But since rhetoric exists to affect the giving of decisions-the hearers decide between one political speaker and another, and a legal verdict is a decision-the orator must not only try to make the argument of his speech demonstrative and worthy of belief; he must also make his own character look right and put his hearers, who are to decide, into the right frame of mind. Particularly in political oratory, but also in lawsuits, it adds much to an orator's influence that his own character should look right and that he should be thought to entertain the right feelings towards his hearers; and also that his hearers themselves should be in just the right frame of mind. That the orator's own character should look right is particularly important in political speaking: that the audience should be in the right frame of mind, in lawsuits. When people are feeling friendly and placable, they think one sort of thing; when they are feeling angry or hostile, they think either something totally different or the same thing with a different intensity: when they feel friendly to the man who comes before them for judgement, they regard him as having done little wrong, if any; when they feel hostile, they take the opposite view. Again, if they are eager for, and have good hopes of, a thing that will be pleasant if it happens, they think that it certainly will happen and be good for them: whereas if they are indifferent or annoyed, they do not think so.

There are three things which inspire confidence in the orator's own character-the three, namely, that induce us to believe a thing apart from any proof of it: good sense, good moral character, and goodwill. False statements and bad advice are due to one or more of the following three causes. Men either form a false opinion through want of good sense; or they form a true opinion, but because of their moral badness do not say what they really think; or finally, they are both sensible and upright, but not well disposed to their hearers, and may fail in consequence to recommend what they know to be the best course. These are the only possible cases. It follows that any one who is thought to have all three of these good qualities will inspire trust in his audience. The way to make ourselves thought to be sensible and morally good must be gathered from the analysis of goodness already given: the way to establish your own goodness is the same as the way to establish that of others. Good will and friendliness of disposition will form part of our discussion of the emotions, to which we must now turn.

The Emotions are all those feelings that so change men as to affect their judgements, and that are also attended by pain or pleasure. Such are anger, pity, fear and the like, with their opposites. We must arrange what we have to say about each of them under three heads. Take, for instance, the emotion of anger: here we must discover (1) what the state of mind of angry people is, (2) who the people are with whom they usually get angry, and (3) on what grounds they get angry with them. It is not enough to know one or even two of these points; unless we know all three, we shall be unable to arouse anger in any one. The same is true of the other emotions. So just as earlier in this work we drew up a list of useful propositions for the orator, let us now proceed in the same way to analyse the subject before us.

Part 2

Anger may be defined as an impulse, accompanied by pain, to a conspicuous revenge for a conspicuous slight directed without justification towards what concerns oneself or towards what concerns one's friends. If this is a proper definition of anger, it must always be felt towards some particular individual, e.g. Cleon, and not 'man' in general. It must be felt because the other has done or intended to do something to him or one of his friends. It must always be attended by a certain pleasure-that which arises from the expectation of revenge. For since nobody aims at what he thinks he cannot attain, the angry man is aiming at what he can attain, and the belief that you will attain your aim is pleasant. Hence it has been well said about wrath,

"Sweeter it is by far than the honeycomb

"dripping with sweetness,

"And spreads through the hearts of men. "

It is also attended by a certain pleasure because the thoughts dwell upon the act of vengeance, and the images then called up cause pleasure, like the images called up in dreams.

Now slighting is the actively entertained opinion of something as obviously of no importance. We think bad things, as well as good ones, have serious importance; and we think the same of anything that tends to produce such things, while those which have little or no such tendency we consider unimportant. There are three kinds of slighting-contempt, spite, and insolence. (1) Contempt is one kind of slighting: you feel contempt for what you consider unimportant, and it is just such things that you slight. (2) Spite is another kind; it is a thwarting another man's wishes, not to get something yourself but to prevent his getting it. The slight arises just from the fact that you do not aim at something for yourself: clearly you do not think that he can do you harm, for then you would be afraid of him instead of slighting him, nor yet that he can do you any good worth mentioning, for then you would be anxious to make friends with him. (3) Insolence is also a form of slighting, since it consists in doing and saying things that cause shame to the victim, not in order that anything may happen to yourself, or because anything has happened to yourself, but simply for the pleasure involved. (Retaliation is not 'insolence', but vengeance.) The cause of the pleasure thus enjoyed by the insolent man is that he thinks himself greatly superior to others when ill-treating them. That is why youths and rich men are insolent; they think themselves superior when they show insolence. One sort of insolence is to rob people of the honour due to them; you certainly slight them thus; for it is the unimportant, for good or evil, that has no honour paid to it. So Achilles says in anger:

"He hath taken my prize for himself

"and hath done me dishonour, "

and

"Like an alien honoured by none, "

meaning that this is why he is angry. A man expects to be specially respected by his inferiors in birth, in capacity, in goodness, and generally in anything in which he is much their superior: as where money is concerned a wealthy man looks for respect from a poor man; where speaking is concerned, the man with a turn for oratory looks for respect from one who cannot speak; the ruler demands the respect of the ruled, and the man who thinks he ought to be a ruler demands the respect of the man whom he thinks he ought to be ruling. Hence it has been said

"Great is the wrath of kings, whose father is Zeus almighty, "

and

"Yea, but his rancour abideth long afterward also, "

their great resentment being due to their great superiority. Then again a man looks for respect from those who he thinks owe him good treatment, and these are the people whom he has treated or is treating well, or means or has meant to treat well, either himself, or through his friends, or through others at his request.

It will be plain by now, from what has been said, (1) in what frame of mind, (2) with what persons, and (3) on what grounds people grow angry. (1) The frame of mind is that of one in which any pain is being felt. In that condition, a man is always aiming at something. Whether, then, another man opposes him either directly in any way, as by preventing him from drinking when he is thirsty, or indirectly, the act appears to him just the same; whether some one works against him, or fails to work with him, or otherwise vexes him while he is in this mood, he is equally angry in all these cases. Hence people who are afflicted by sickness or poverty or love or thirst or any other unsatisfied desires are prone to anger and easily roused: especially against those who slight their present distress. Thus a sick man is angered by disregard of his illness, a poor man by disregard of his poverty, a man aging war by disregard of the war he is waging, a lover by disregard of his love, and so throughout, any other sort of slight being enough if special slights are wanting. Each man is predisposed, by the emotion now controlling him, to his own particular anger. Further, we are angered if we happen to be expecting a contrary result: for a quite unexpected evil is specially painful, just as the quite unexpected fulfilment of our wishes is specially pleasant. Hence it is plain what seasons, times, conditions, and periods of life tend to stir men easily to anger, and where and when this will happen; and it is plain that the more we are under these conditions the more easily we are stirred.

These, then, are the frames of mind in which men are easily stirred to anger. The persons with whom we get angry are those who laugh, mock, or jeer at us, for such conduct is insolent. Also those who inflict injuries upon us that are marks of insolence. These injuries must be such as are neither retaliatory nor profitable to the doers: for only then will they be felt to be due to insolence. Also those who speak ill of us, and show contempt for us, in connexion with the things we ourselves most care about: thus those who are eager to win fame as philosophers get angry with those who show contempt for their philosophy; those who pride themselves upon their appearance get angry with those who show contempt for their appearance and so on in other cases. We feel particularly angry on this account if we suspect that we are in fact, or that people think we are, lacking completely or to any effective extent in the qualities in question. For when we are convinced that we excel in the qualities for which we are jeered at, we can ignore the jeering. Again, we are angrier with our friends than with other people, since we feel that our friends ought to treat us well and not badly. We are angry with those who have usually treated us with honour or regard, if a change comes and they behave to us otherwise: for we think that they feel contempt for us, or they would still be behaving as they did before. And with those who do not return our kindnesses or fail to return them adequately, and with those who oppose us though they are our inferiors: for all such persons seem to feel contempt for us; those who oppose us seem to think us inferior to themselves, and those who do not return our kindnesses seem to think that those kindnesses were conferred by inferiors. And we feel particularly angry with men of no account at all, if they slight us. For, by our hypothesis, the anger caused by the slight is felt towards people who are not justified in slighting us, and our inferiors are not thus justified. Again, we feel angry with friends if they do not speak well of us or treat us well; and still more, if they do the contrary; or if they do not perceive our needs, which is why Plexippus is angry with Meleager in Antiphon's play; for this want of perception shows that they are slighting us-we do not fail to perceive the needs of those for whom we care. Again we are angry with those who rejoice at our misfortunes or simply keep cheerful in the midst of our misfortunes, since this shows that they either hate us or are slighting us. Also with those who are indifferent to the pain they give us: this is why we get angry with bringers of bad news. And with those who listen to stories about us or keep on looking at our weaknesses; this seems like either slighting us or hating us; for those who love us share in all our distresses and it must distress any one to keep on looking at his own weaknesses. Further, with those who slight us before five classes of people: namely, (1) our rivals, (2) those whom we admire, (3) those whom we wish to admire us, (4) those for whom we feel reverence, (5) those who feel reverence for us: if any one slights us before such persons, we feel particularly angry. Again, we feel angry with those who slight us in connexion with what we are as honourable men bound to champion-our parents, children, wives, or subjects. And with those who do not return a favour, since such a slight is unjustifiable. Also with those who reply with humorous levity when we are speaking seriously, for such behaviour indicates contempt. And with those who treat us less well than they treat everybody else; it is another mark of contempt that they should think we do not deserve what every one else deserves. Forgetfulness, too, causes anger, as when our own names are forgotten, trifling as this may be; since forgetfulness is felt to be another sign that we are being slighted; it is due to negligence, and to neglect us is to slight us.

The persons with whom we feel anger, the frame of mind in which we feel it, and the reasons why we feel it, have now all been set forth. Clearly the orator will have to speak so as to bring his hearers into a frame of mind that will dispose them to anger, and to represent his adversaries as open to such charges and possessed of such qualities as do make people angry.

Part 3

Since growing calm is the opposite of growing angry, and calmness the opposite of anger, we must ascertain in what frames of mind men are calm, towards whom they feel calm, and by what means they are made so. Growing calm may be defined as a settling down or quieting of anger. Now we get angry with those who slight us; and since slighting is a voluntary act, it is plain that we feel calm towards those who do nothing of the kind, or who do or seem to do it involuntarily. Also towards those who intended to do the opposite of what they did do. Also towards those who treat themselves as they have treated us: since no one can be supposed to slight himself. Also towards those who admit their fault and are sorry: since we accept their grief at what they have done as satisfaction, and cease to be angry. The punishment of servants shows this: those who contradict us and deny their offence we punish all the more, but we cease to be incensed against those who agree that they deserved their punishment. The reason is that it is shameless to deny what is obvious, and those who are shameless towards us slight us and show contempt for us: anyhow, we do not feel shame before those of whom we are thoroughly contemptuous. Also we feel calm towards those who humble themselves before us and do not gainsay us; we feel that they thus admit themselves our inferiors, and inferiors feel fear, and nobody can slight any one so long as he feels afraid of him. That our anger ceases towards those who humble themselves before us is shown even by dogs, who do not bite people when they sit down. We also feel calm towards those who are serious when we are serious, because then we feel that we are treated seriously and not contemptuously. Also towards those who have done us more kindnesses than we have done them. Also towards those who pray to us and beg for mercy, since they humble themselves by doing so. Also towards those who do not insult or mock at or slight any one at all, or not any worthy person or any one like ourselves. In general, the things that make us calm may be inferred by seeing what the opposites are of those that make us angry. We are not angry with people we fear or respect, as long as we fear or respect them; you cannot be afraid of a person and also at the same time angry with him. Again, we feel no anger, or comparatively little, with those who have done what they did through anger: we do not feel that they have done it from a wish to slight us, for no one slights people when angry with them, since slighting is painless, and anger is painful. Nor do we grow angry with those who reverence us.

As to the frame of mind that makes people calm, it is plainly the opposite to that which makes them angry, as when they are amusing themselves or laughing or feasting; when they are feeling prosperous or successful or satisfied; when, in fine, they are enjoying freedom from pain, or inoffensive pleasure, or justifiable hope. Also when time has passed and their anger is no longer fresh, for time puts an end to anger. And vengeance previously taken on one person puts an end to even greater anger felt against another person. Hence Philocrates, being asked by some one, at a time when the public was angry with him, 'Why don't you defend yourself?' did right to reply, 'The time is not yet.' 'Why, when is the time?' 'When I see someone else calumniated.' For men become calm when they have spent their anger on somebody else. This happened in the case of Ergophilus: though the people were more irritated against him than against Callisthenes, they acquitted him because they had condemned Callisthenes to death the day before. Again, men become calm if they have convicted the offender; or if he has already suffered worse things than they in their anger would have themselves inflicted upon him; for they feel as if they were already avenged. Or if they feel that they themselves are in the wrong and are suffering justly (for anger is not excited by what is just), since men no longer think then that they are suffering without justification; and anger, as we have seen, means this. Hence we ought always to inflict a preliminary punishment in words: if that is done, even slaves are less aggrieved by the actual punishment. We also feel calm if we think that the offender will not see that he is punished on our account and because of the way he has treated us. For anger has to do with individuals. This is plain from the definition. Hence the poet has well written:

"Say that it was Odysseus, sacker of cities, "

implying that Odysseus would not have considered himself avenged unless the Cyclops perceived both by whom and for what he had been blinded. Consequently we do not get angry with any one who cannot be aware of our anger, and in particular we cease to be angry with people once they are dead, for we feel that the worst has been done to them, and that they will neither feel pain nor anything else that we in our anger aim at making them feel. And therefore the poet has well made Apollo say, in order to put a stop to the anger of Achilles against the dead Hector,

"For behold in his fury he doeth despite to the senseless clay. "

It is now plain that when you wish to calm others you must draw upon these lines of argument; you must put your hearers into the corresponding frame of mind, and represent those with whom they are angry as formidable, or as worthy of reverence, or as benefactors, or as involuntary agents, or as much distressed at what they have done.

Part 4

Let us now turn to Friendship and Enmity, and ask towards whom these feelings are entertained, and why. We will begin by defining and friendly feeling. We may describe friendly feeling towards any one as wishing for him what you believe to be good things, not for your own sake but for his, and being inclined, so far as you can, to bring these things about. A friend is one who feels thus and excites these feelings in return: those who think they feel thus towards each other think themselves friends. This being assumed, it follows that your friend is the sort of man who shares your pleasure in what is good and your pain in what is unpleasant, for your sake and for no other reason. This pleasure and pain of his will be the token of his good wishes for you, since we all feel glad at getting what we wish for, and pained at getting what we do not. Those, then, are friends to whom the same things are good and evil; and those who are, moreover, friendly or unfriendly to the same people; for in that case they must have the same wishes, and thus by wishing for each other what they wish for themselves, they show themselves each other's friends.

Again, we feel friendly to those who have treated us well, either ourselves or those we care for, whether on a large scale, or readily, or at some particular crisis; provided it was for our own sake. And also to those who we think wish to treat us well. And also to our friends' friends, and to those who like, or are liked by, those whom we like ourselves. And also to those who are enemies to those whose enemies we are, and dislike, or are disliked by, those whom we dislike. For all such persons think the things good which we think good, so that they wish what is good for us; and this, as we saw, is what friends must do. And also to those who are willing to treat us well where money or our personal safety is concerned: and therefore we value those who are liberal, brave, or just. The just we consider to be those who do not live on others; which means those who work for their living, especially farmers and others who work with their own hands.

We also like temperate men, because they are not unjust to others; and, for the same reason, those who mind their own business. And also those whose friends we wish to be, if it is plain that they wish to be our friends: such are the morally good, and those well thought of by every one, by the best men, or by those whom we admire or who admire us. And also those with whom it is pleasant to live and spend our days: such are the good-tempered, and those who are not too ready to show us our mistakes, and those who are not cantankerous or quarrelsome-such people are always wanting to fight us, and those who fight us we feel wish for the opposite of what we wish for ourselves-and those who have the tact to make and take a joke; here both parties have the same object in view, when they can stand being made fun of as well as do it prettily themselves.

And we also feel friendly towards those who praise such good qualities as we possess, and especially if they praise the good qualities that we are not too sure we do possess. And towards those who are cleanly in their person, their dress, and all their way of life. And towards those who do not reproach us with what we have done amiss to them or they have done to help us, for both actions show a tendency to criticize us. And towards those who do not nurse grudges or store up grievances, but are always ready to make friends again; for we take it that they will behave to us just as we find them behaving to every one else. And towards those who are not evil speakers and who are aware of neither their neighbours' bad points nor our own, but of our good ones only, as a good man always will be. And towards those who do not try to thwart us when we are angry or in earnest, which would mean being ready to fight us. And towards those who have some serious feeling towards us, such as admiration for us, or belief in our goodness, or pleasure in our company; especially if they feel like this about qualities in us for which we especially wish to be admired, esteemed, or liked. And towards those who are like ourselves in character and occupation, provided they do not get in our way or gain their living from the same source as we do-for then it will be a case of 'potter against potter':

"Potter to potter and builder to builder begrudge their reward. "

And those who desire the same things as we desire, if it is possible for us both to share them together; otherwise the same trouble arises here too. And towards those with whom we are on such terms that, while we respect their opinions, we need not blush before them for doing what is conventionally wrong: as well as towards those before whom we should be ashamed to do anything really wrong. Again, our rivals, and those whom we should like to envy us--though without ill-feeling--either we like these people or at least we wish them to like us. And we feel friendly towards those whom we help to secure good for themselves, provided we are not likely to suffer heavily by it ourselves. And those who feel as friendly to us when we are not with them as when we are-which is why all men feel friendly towards those who are faithful to their dead friends. And, speaking generally, towards those who are really fond of their friends and do not desert them in trouble; of all good men, we feel most friendly to those who show their goodness as friends. Also towards those who are honest with us, including those who will tell us of their own weak points: it has just said that with our friends we are not ashamed of what is conventionally wrong, and if we do have this feeling, we do not love them; if therefore we do not have it, it looks as if we did love them. We also like those with whom we do not feel frightened or uncomfortable-nobody can like a man of whom he feels frightened. Friendship has various forms-comradeship, intimacy, kinship, and so on.

Things that cause friendship are: doing kindnesses; doing them unasked; and not proclaiming the fact when they are done, which shows that they were done for our own sake and not for some other reason.

Enmity and Hatred should clearly be studied by reference to their opposites. Enmity may be produced by anger or spite or calumny. Now whereas anger arises from offences against oneself, enmity may arise even without that; we may hate people merely because of what we take to be their character. Anger is always concerned with individuals-a Callias or a Socrates-whereas hatred is directed also against classes: we all hate any thief and any informer. Moreover, anger can be cured by time; but hatred cannot. The one aims at giving pain to its object, the other at doing him harm; the angry man wants his victims to feel; the hater does not mind whether they feel or not. All painful things are felt; but the greatest evils, injustice and folly, are the least felt, since their presence causes no pain. And anger is accompanied by pain, hatred is not; the angry man feels pain, but the hater does not. Much may happen to make the angry man pity those who offend him, but the hater under no circumstances wishes to pity a man whom he has once hated: for the one would have the offenders suffer for what they have done; the other would have them cease to exist.

It is plain from all this that we can prove people to be friends or enemies; if they are not, we can make them out to be so; if they claim to be so, we can refute their claim; and if it is disputed whether an action was due to anger or to hatred, we can attribute it to whichever of these we prefer.

Part 5

To turn next to Fear, what follows will show things and persons of which, and the states of mind in which, we feel afraid. Fear may be defined as a pain or disturbance due to a mental picture of some destructive or painful evil in the future. Of destructive or painful evils only; for there are some evils, e.g. wickedness or stupidity, the prospect of which does not frighten us: I mean only such as amount to great pains or losses. And even these only if they appear not remote but so near as to be imminent: we do not fear things that are a very long way off: for instance, we all know we shall die, but we are not troubled thereby, because death is not close at hand. From this definition it will follow that fear is caused by whatever we feel has great power of destroying or of harming us in ways that tend to cause us great pain. Hence the very indications of such things are terrible, making us feel that the terrible thing itself is close at hand; the approach of what is terrible is just what we mean by 'danger'. Such indications are the enmity and anger of people who have power to do something to us; for it is plain that they have the will to do it, and so they are on the point of doing it. Also injustice in possession of power; for it is the unjust man's will to do evil that makes him unjust. Also outraged virtue in possession of power; for it is plain that, when outraged, it always has the will to retaliate, and now it has the power to do so. Also fear felt by those who have the power to do something to us, since such persons are sure to be ready to do it. And since most men tend to be bad-slaves to greed, and cowards in danger-it is, as a rule, a terrible thing to be at another man's mercy; and therefore, if we have done anything horrible, those in the secret terrify us with the thought that they may betray or desert us. And those who can do us wrong are terrible to us when we are liable to be wronged; for as a rule men do wrong to others whenever they have the power to do it. And those who have been wronged, or believe themselves to be wronged, are terrible; for they are always looking out for their opportunity. Also those who have done people wrong, if they possess power, since they stand in fear of retaliation: we have already said that wickedness possessing power is terrible. Again, our rivals for a thing cause us fear when we cannot both have it at once; for we are always at war with such men. We also fear those who are to be feared by stronger people than ourselves: if they can hurt those stronger people, still more can they hurt us; and, for the same reason, we fear those whom those stronger people are actually afraid of. Also those who have destroyed people stronger than we are. Also those who are attacking people weaker than we are: either they are already formidable, or they will be so when they have thus grown stronger. Of those we have wronged, and of our enemies or rivals, it is not the passionate and outspoken whom we have to fear, but the quiet, dissembling, unscrupulous; since we never know when they are upon us, we can never be sure they are at a safe distance. All terrible things are more terrible if they give us no chance of retrieving a blunder either no chance at all, or only one that depends on our enemies and not ourselves. Those things are also worse which we cannot, or cannot easily, help. Speaking generally, anything causes us to feel fear that when it happens to, or threatens, others cause us to feel pity.

The above are, roughly, the chief things that are terrible and are feared. Let us now describe the conditions under which we ourselves feel fear. If fear is associated with the expectation that something destructive will happen to us, plainly nobody will be afraid who believes nothing can happen to him; we shall not fear things that we believe cannot happen to us, nor people who we believe cannot inflict them upon us; nor shall we be afraid at times when we think ourselves safe from them. It follows therefore that fear is felt by those who believe something to be likely to happen to them, at the hands of particular persons, in a particular form, and at a particular time. People do not believe this when they are, or think they a are, in the midst of great prosperity, and are in consequence insolent, contemptuous, and reckless-the kind of character produced by wealth, physical strength, abundance of friends, power: nor yet when they feel they have experienced every kind of horror already and have grown callous about the future, like men who are being flogged and are already nearly dead-if they are to feel the anguish of uncertainty, there must be some faint expectation of escape. This appears from the fact that fear sets us thinking what can be done, which of course nobody does when things are hopeless. Consequently, when it is advisable that the audience should be frightened, the orator must make them feel that they really are in danger of something, pointing out that it has happened to others who were stronger than they are, and is happening, or has happened, to people like themselves, at the hands of unexpected people, in an unexpected form, and at an unexpected time.

Having now seen the nature of fear, and of the things that cause it, and the various states of mind in which it is felt, we can also see what Confidence is, about what things we feel it, and under what conditions. It is the opposite of fear, and what causes it is the opposite of what causes fear; it is, therefore, the expectation associated with a mental picture of the nearness of what keeps us safe and the absence or remoteness of what is terrible: it may be due either to the near presence of what inspires confidence or to the absence of what causes alarm. We feel it if we can take steps-many, or important, or both-to cure or prevent trouble; if we have neither wronged others nor been wronged by them; if we have either no rivals at all or no strong ones; if our rivals who are strong are our friends or have treated us well or been treated well by us; or if those whose interest is the same as ours are the more numerous party, or the stronger, or both.

As for our own state of mind, we feel confidence if we believe we have often succeeded and never suffered reverses, or have often met danger and escaped it safely. For there are two reasons why human beings face danger calmly: they may have no experience of it, or they may have means to deal with it: thus when in danger at sea people may feel confident about what will happen either because they have no experience of bad weather, or because their experience gives them the means of dealing with it. We also feel confident whenever there is nothing to terrify other people like ourselves, or people weaker than ourselves, or people than whom we believe ourselves to be stronger-and we believe this if we have conquered them, or conquered others who are as strong as they are, or stronger. Also if we believe ourselves superior to our rivals in the number and importance of the advantages that make men formidable-wealth, physical strength, strong bodies of supporters, extensive territory, and the possession of all, or the most important, appliances of war. Also if we have wronged no one, or not many, or not those of whom we are afraid; and generally, if our relations with the gods are satisfactory, as will be shown especially by signs and oracles. The fact is that anger makes us confident-that anger is excited by our knowledge that we are not the wrongers but the wronged, and that the divine power is always supposed to be on the side of the wronged. Also when, at the outset of an enterprise, we believe that we cannot and shall not fail, or that we shall succeed completely.-So much for the causes of fear and confidence.

Part 6

We now turn to Shame and Shamelessness; what follows will explain the things that cause these feelings, and the persons before whom, and the states of mind under which, they are felt. Shame may be defined as pain or disturbance in regard to bad things, whether present, past, or future, which seem likely to involve us in discredit; and shamelessness as contempt or indifference in regard to these same bad things. If this definition be granted, it follows that we feel shame at such bad things as we think are disgraceful to ourselves or to those we care for. These evils are, in the first place, those due to moral badness. Such are throwing away one's shield or taking to flight; for these bad things are due to cowardice. Also, withholding a deposit or otherwise wronging people about money; for these acts are due to injustice. Also, having carnal intercourse with forbidden persons, at wrong times, or in wrong places; for these things are due to licentiousness. Also, making profit in petty or disgraceful ways, or out of helpless persons, e.g. the poor, or the dead-whence the proverb 'He would pick a corpse's pocket'; for all this is due to low greed and meanness. Also, in money matters, giving less help than you might, or none at all, or accepting help from those worse off than yourself; so also borrowing when it will seem like begging; begging when it will seem like asking the return of a favour; asking such a return when it will seem like begging; praising a man in order that it may seem like begging; and going on begging in spite of failure: all such actions are tokens of meanness. Also, praising people to their face, and praising extravagantly a man's good points and glozing over his weaknesses, and showing extravagant sympathy with his grief when you are in his presence, and all that sort of thing; all this shows the disposition of a flatterer. Also, refusing to endure hardships that are endured by people who are older, more delicately brought up, of higher rank, or generally less capable of endurance than ourselves: for all this shows effeminacy. Also, accepting benefits, especially accepting them often, from another man, and then abusing him for conferring them: all this shows a mean, ignoble disposition. Also, talking incessantly about yourself, making loud professions, and appropriating the merits of others; for this is due to boastfulness. The same is true of the actions due to any of the other forms of badness of moral character, of the tokens of such badness, &c.: they are all disgraceful and shameless. Another sort of bad thing at which we feel shame is, lacking a share in the honourable things shared by every one else, or by all or nearly all who are like ourselves. By 'those like ourselves' I mean those of our own race or country or age or family, and generally those who are on our own level. Once we are on a level with others, it is a disgrace to be, say, less well educated than they are; and so with other advantages: all the more so, in each case, if it is seen to be our own fault: wherever we are ourselves to blame for our present, past, or future circumstances, it follows at once that this is to a greater extent due to our moral badness. We are moreover ashamed of having done to us, having had done, or being about to have done to us acts that involve us in dishonour and reproach; as when we surrender our persons, or lend ourselves to vile deeds, e.g. when we submit to outrage. And acts of yielding to the lust of others are shameful whether willing or unwilling (yielding to force being an instance of unwillingness), since unresisting submission to them is due to unmanliness or cowardice.

These things, and others like them, are what cause the feeling of shame. Now since shame is a mental picture of disgrace, in which we shrink from the disgrace itself and not from its consequences, and we only care what opinion is held of us because of the people who form that opinion, it follows that the people before whom we feel shame are those whose opinion of us matters to us. Such persons are: those who admire us, those whom we admire, those by whom we wish to be admired, those with whom we are competing, and those whose opinion of us we respect. We admire those, and wish those to admire us, who possess any good thing that is highly esteemed; or from whom we are very anxious to get something that they are able to give us-as a lover feels. We compete with our equals. We respect, as true, the views of sensible people, such as our elders and those who have been well educated. And we feel more shame about a thing if it is done openly, before all men's eyes. Hence the proverb, 'shame dwells in the eyes'. For this reason we feel most shame before those who will always be with us and those who notice what we do, since in both cases eyes are upon us. We also feel it before those not open to the same imputation as ourselves: for it is plain that their opinions about it are the opposite of ours. Also before those who are hard on any one whose conduct they think wrong; for what a man does himself, he is said not to resent when his neighbours do it: so that of course he does resent their doing what he does not do himself. And before those who are likely to tell everybody about you; not telling others is as good as not believing you wrong. People are likely to tell others about you if you have wronged them, since they are on the look out to harm you; or if they speak evil of everybody, for those who attack the innocent will be still more ready to attack the guilty. And before those whose main occupation is with their neighbours' failings-people like satirists and writers of comedy; these are really a kind of evil-speakers and tell-tales. And before those who have never yet known us come to grief, since their attitude to us has amounted to admiration so far: that is why we feel ashamed to refuse those a favour who ask one for the first time-we have not as yet lost credit with them. Such are those who are just beginning to wish to be our friends; for they have seen our best side only (hence the appropriateness of Euripides' reply to the Syracusans): and such also are those among our old acquaintances who know nothing to our discredit. And we are ashamed not merely of the actual shameful conduct mentioned, but also of the evidences of it: not merely, for example, of actual sexual intercourse, but also of its evidences; and not merely of disgraceful acts but also of disgraceful talk. Similarly we feel shame not merely in presence of the persons mentioned but also of those who will tell them what we have done, such as their servants or friends. And, generally, we feel no shame before those upon whose opinions we quite look down as untrustworthy (no one feels shame before small children or animals); nor are we ashamed of the same things before intimates as before strangers, but before the former of what seem genuine faults, before the latter of what seem conventional ones.

The conditions under which we shall feel shame are these: first, having people related to us like those before whom, as has been said, we feel shame. These are, as was stated, persons whom we admire, or who admire us, or by whom we wish to be admired, or from whom we desire some service that we shall not obtain if we forfeit their good opinion. These persons may be actually looking on (as Cydias represented them in his speech on land assignments in Samos, when he told the Athenians to imagine the Greeks to be standing all around them, actually seeing the way they voted and not merely going to hear about it afterwards): or again they may be near at hand, or may be likely to find out about what we do. This is why in misfortune we do not wish to be seen by those who once wished themselves like us; for such a feeling implies admiration. And men feel shame when they have acts or exploits to their credit on which they are bringing dishonour, whether these are their own, or those of their ancestors, or those of other persons with whom they have some close connexion. Generally, we feel shame before those for whose own misconduct we should also feel it-those already mentioned; those who take us as their models; those whose teachers or advisers we have been; or other people, it may be, like ourselves, whose rivals we are. For there are many things that shame before such people makes us do or leave undone. And we feel more shame when we are likely to be continually seen by, and go about under the eyes of, those who know of our disgrace. Hence, when Antiphon the poet was to be cudgelled to death by order of Dionysius, and saw those who were to perish with him covering their faces as they went through the gates, he said, 'Why do you cover your faces? Is it lest some of these spectators should see you to-morrow?'

So much for Shame; to understand Shamelessness, we need only consider the converse cases, and plainly we shall have all we need.

Part 7

To take Kindness next: the definition of it will show us towards whom it is felt, why, and in what frames of mind. Kindness-under the influence of which a man is said to 'be kind' may be defined as helpfulness towards some one in need, not in return for anything, nor for the advantage of the helper himself, but for that of the person helped. Kindness is great if shown to one who is in great need, or who needs what is important and hard to get, or who needs it at an important and difficult crisis; or if the helper is the only, the first, or the chief person to give the help. Natural cravings constitute such needs; and in particular cravings, accompanied by pain, for what is not being attained. The appetites are cravings for this kind: sexual desire, for instance, and those which arise during bodily injuries and in dangers; for appetite is active both in danger and in pain. Hence those who stand by us in poverty or in banishment, even if they do not help us much, are yet really kind to us, because our need is great and the occasion pressing; for instance, the man who gave the mat in the Lyceum. The helpfulness must therefore meet, preferably, just this kind of need; and failing just this kind, some other kind as great or greater. We now see to whom, why, and under what conditions kindness is shown; and these facts must form the basis of our arguments. We must show that the persons helped are, or have been, in such pain and need as has been described, and that their helpers gave, or are giving, the kind of help described, in the kind of need described. We can also see how to eliminate the idea of kindness and make our opponents appear unkind: we may maintain that they are being or have been helpful simply to promote their own interest-this, as has been stated, is not kindness; or that their action was accidental, or was forced upon them; or that they were not doing a favour, but merely returning one, whether they know this or not-in either case the action is a mere return, and is therefore not a kindness even if the doer does not know how the case stands. In considering this subject we must look at all the categories: an act may be an act of kindness because (1) it is a particular thing, (2) it has a particular magnitude or (3) quality, or (4) is done at a particular time or (5) place. As evidence of the want of kindness, we may point out that a smaller service had been refused to the man in need; or that the same service, or an equal or greater one, has been given to his enemies; these facts show that the service in question was not done for the sake of the person helped. Or we may point out that the thing desired was worthless and that the helper knew it: no one will admit that he is in need of what is worthless.

Part 8

So much for Kindness and Unkindness. Let us now consider Pity, asking ourselves what things excite pity, and for what persons, and in what states of our mind pity is felt. Pity may be defined as a feeling of pain caused by the sight of some evil, destructive or painful, which befalls one who does not deserve it, and which we might expect to befall ourselves or some friend of ours, and moreover to befall us soon. In order to feel pity, we must obviously be capable of supposing that some evil may happen to us or some friend of ours, and moreover some such evil as is stated in our definition or is more or less of that kind. It is therefore not felt by those completely ruined, who suppose that no further evil can befall them, since the worst has befallen them already; nor by those who imagine themselves immensely fortunate-their feeling is rather presumptuous insolence, for when they think they possess all the good things of life, it is clear that the impossibility of evil befalling them will be included, this being one of the good things in question. Those who think evil may befall them are such as have already had it befall them and have safely escaped from it; elderly men, owing to their good sense and their experience; weak men, especially men inclined to cowardice; and also educated people, since these can take long views. Also those who have parents living, or children, or wives; for these are our own, and the evils mentioned above may easily befall them. And those who neither moved by any courageous emotion such as anger or confidence (these emotions take no account of the future), nor by a disposition to presumptuous insolence (insolent men, too, take no account of the possibility that something evil will happen to them), nor yet by great fear (panic-stricken people do not feel pity, because they are taken up with what is happening to themselves); only those feel pity who are between these two extremes. In order to feel pity we must also believe in the goodness of at least some people; if you think nobody good, you will believe that everybody deserves evil fortune. And, generally, we feel pity whenever we are in the condition of remembering that similar misfortunes have happened to us or ours, or expecting them to happen in the future.

So much for the mental conditions under which we feel pity. What we pity is stated clearly in the definition. All unpleasant and painful things excite pity if they tend to destroy pain and annihilate; and all such evils as are due to chance, if they are serious. The painful and destructive evils are: death in its various forms, bodily injuries and afflictions, old age, diseases, lack of food. The evils due to chance are: friendlessness, scarcity of friends (it is a pitiful thing to be torn away from friends and companions), deformity, weakness, mutilation; evil coming from a source from which good ought to have come; and the frequent repetition of such misfortunes. Also the coming of good when the worst has happened: e.g. the arrival of the Great King's gifts for Diopeithes after his death. Also that either no good should have befallen a man at all, or that he should not be able to enjoy it when it has.

The grounds, then, on which we feel pity are these or like these. The people we pity are: those whom we know, if only they are not very closely related to us-in that case we feel about them as if we were in danger ourselves. For this reason Amasis did not weep, they say, at the sight of his son being led to death, but did weep when he saw his friend begging: the latter sight was pitiful, the former terrible, and the terrible is different from the pitiful; it tends to cast out pity, and often helps to produce the opposite of pity. Again, we feel pity when the danger is near ourselves. Also we pity those who are like us in age, character, disposition, social standing, or birth; for in all these cases it appears more likely that the same misfortune may befall us also. Here too we have to remember the general principle that what we fear for ourselves excites our pity when it happens to others. Further, since it is when the sufferings of others are close to us that they excite our pity (we cannot remember what disasters happened a hundred centuries ago, nor look forward to what will happen a hundred centuries hereafter, and therefore feel little pity, if any, for such things): it follows that those who heighten the effect of their words with suitable gestures, tones, dress, and dramatic action generally, are especially successful in exciting pity: they thus put the disasters before our eyes, and make them seem close to us, just coming or just past. Anything that has just happened, or is going to happen soon, is particularly piteous: so too therefore are the tokens and the actions of sufferers-the garments and the like of those who have already suffered; the words and the like of those actually suffering-of those, for instance, who are on the point of death. Most piteous of all is it when, in such times of trial, the victims are persons of noble character: whenever they are so, our pity is especially excited, because their innocence, as well as the setting of their misfortunes before our eyes, makes their misfortunes seem close to ourselves.

Part 9

Most directly opposed to pity is the feeling called Indignation. Pain at unmerited good fortune is, in one sense, opposite to pain at unmerited bad fortune, and is due to the same moral qualities. Both feelings are associated with good moral character; it is our duty both to feel sympathy and pity for unmerited distress, and to feel indignation at unmerited prosperity; for whatever is undeserved is unjust, and that is why we ascribe indignation even to the gods. It might indeed be thought that envy is similarly opposed to pity, on the ground that envy it closely akin to indignation, or even the same thing. But it is not the same. It is true that it also is a disturbing pain excited by the prosperity of others. But it is excited not by the prosperity of the undeserving but by that of people who are like us or equal with us. The two feelings have this in common, that they must be due not to some untoward thing being likely to befall ourselves, but only to what is happening to our neighbour. The feeling ceases to be envy in the one case and indignation in the other, and becomes fear, if the pain and disturbance are due to the prospect of something bad for ourselves as the result of the other man's good fortune. The feelings of pity and indignation will obviously be attended by the converse feelings of satisfaction. If you are pained by the unmerited distress of others, you will be pleased, or at least not pained, by their merited distress. Thus no good man can be pained by the punishment of parricides or murderers. These are things we are bound to rejoice at, as we must at the prosperity of the deserving; both these things are just, and both give pleasure to any honest man, since he cannot help expecting that what has happened to a man like him will happen to him too. All these feelings are associated with the same type of moral character. And their contraries are associated with the contrary type; the man who is delighted by others' misfortunes is identical with the man who envies others' prosperity. For any one who is pained by the occurrence or existence of a given thing must be pleased by that thing's non-existence or destruction. We can now see that all these feelings tend to prevent pity (though they differ among themselves, for the reasons given), so that all are equally useful for neutralizing an appeal to pity.

We will first consider Indignation-reserving the other emotions for subsequent discussion-and ask with whom, on what grounds, and in what states of mind we may be indignant. These questions are really answered by what has been said already. Indignation is pain caused by the sight of undeserved good fortune. It is, then, plain to begin with that there are some forms of good the sight of which cannot cause it. Thus a man may be just or brave, or acquire moral goodness: but we shall not be indignant with him for that reason, any more than we shall pity him for the contrary reason. Indignation is roused by the sight of wealth, power, and the like-by all those things, roughly speaking, which are deserved by good men and by those who possess the goods of nature-noble birth, beauty, and so on. Again, what is long established seems akin to what exists by nature; and therefore we feel more indignation at those possessing a given good if they have as a matter of fact only just got it and the prosperity it brings with it. The newly rich give more offence than those whose wealth is of long standing and inherited. The same is true of those who have office or power, plenty of friends, a fine family, &c. We feel the same when these advantages of theirs secure them others. For here again, the newly rich give us more offence by obtaining office through their riches than do those whose wealth is of long standing; and so in all other cases. The reason is that what the latter have is felt to be really their own, but what the others have is not; what appears to have been always what it is is regarded as real, and so the possessions of the newly rich do not seem to be really their own. Further, it is not any and every man that deserves any given kind of good; there is a certain correspondence and appropriateness in such things; thus it is appropriate for brave men, not for just men, to have fine weapons, and for men of family, not for parvenus, to make distinguished marriages. Indignation may therefore properly be felt when any one gets what is not appropriate for him, though he may be a good man enough. It may also be felt when any one sets himself up against his superior, especially against his superior in some particular respect-whence the lines

"Only from battle he shrank with Aias Telamon's son;

"Zeus had been angered with him,

"had he fought with a mightier one; "

but also, even apart from that, when the inferior in any sense contends with his superior; a musician, for instance, with a just man, for justice is a finer thing than music.

Enough has been said to make clear the grounds on which, and the persons against whom, Indignation is felt-they are those mentioned, and others like him. As for the people who feel it; we feel it if we do ourselves deserve the greatest possible goods and moreover have them, for it is an injustice that those who are not our equals should have been held to deserve as much as we have. Or, secondly, we feel it if we are really good and honest people; our judgement is then sound, and we loathe any kind of injustice. Also if we are ambitious and eager to gain particular ends, especially if we are ambitious for what others are getting without deserving to get it. And, generally, if we think that we ourselves deserve a thing and that others do not, we are disposed to be indignant with those others so far as that thing is concerned. Hence servile, worthless, unambitious persons are not inclined to Indignation, since there is nothing they can believe themselves to deserve.

From all this it is plain what sort of men those are at whose misfortunes, distresses, or failures we ought to feel pleased, or at least not pained: by considering the facts described we see at once what their contraries are. If therefore our speech puts the judges in such a frame of mind as that indicated and shows that those who claim pity on certain definite grounds do not deserve to secure pity but do deserve not to secure it, it will be impossible for the judges to feel pity.

Part 10

To take Envy next: we can see on what grounds, against what persons, and in what states of mind we feel it. Envy is pain at the sight of such good fortune as consists of the good things already mentioned; we feel it towards our equals; not with the idea of getting something for ourselves, but because the other people have it. We shall feel it if we have, or think we have, equals; and by 'equals' I mean equals in birth, relationship, age, disposition, distinction, or wealth. We feel envy also if we fall but a little short of having everything; which is why people in high place and prosperity feel it-they think every one else is taking what belongs to themselves. Also if we are exceptionally distinguished for some particular thing, and especially if that thing is wisdom or good fortune. Ambitious men are more envious than those who are not. So also those who profess wisdom; they are ambitious to be thought wise. Indeed, generally, those who aim at a reputation for anything are envious on this particular point. And small-minded men are envious, for everything seems great to them. The good things which excite envy have already been mentioned. The deeds or possessions which arouse the love of reputation and honour and the desire for fame, and the various gifts of fortune, are almost all subject to envy; and particularly if we desire the thing ourselves, or think we are entitled to it, or if having it puts us a little above others, or not having it a little below them. It is clear also what kind of people we envy; that was included in what has been said already: we envy those who are near us in time, place, age, or reputation. Hence the line:

"Ay, kin can even be jealous of their kin. "

Also our fellow-competitors, who are indeed the people just mentioned-we do not compete with men who lived a hundred centuries ago, or those not yet born, or the dead, or those who dwell near the Pillars of Hercules, or those whom, in our opinion or that of others, we take to be far below us or far above us. So too we compete with those who follow the same ends as ourselves: we compete with our rivals in sport or in love, and generally with those who are after the same things; and it is therefore these whom we are bound to envy beyond all others. Hence the saying:

"Potter against potter. "

We also envy those whose possession of or success in a thing is a reproach to us: these are our neighbours and equals; for it is clear that it is our own fault we have missed the good thing in question; this annoys us, and excites envy in us. We also envy those who have what we ought to have, or have got what we did have once. Hence old men envy younger men, and those who have spent much envy those who have spent little on the same thing. And men who have not got a thing, or not got it yet, envy those who have got it quickly. We can also see what things and what persons give pleasure to envious people, and in what states of mind they feel it: the states of mind in which they feel pain are those under which they will feel pleasure in the contrary things. If therefore we ourselves with whom the decision rests are put into an envious state of mind, and those for whom our pity, or the award of something desirable, is claimed are such as have been described, it is obvious that they will win no pity from us.

Part 11

We will next consider Emulation, showing in what follows its causes and objects, and the state of mind in which it is felt. Emulation is pain caused by seeing the presence, in persons whose nature is like our own, of good things that are highly valued and are possible for ourselves to acquire; but it is felt not because others have these goods, but because we have not got them ourselves. It is therefore a good feeling felt by good persons, whereas envy is a bad feeling felt by bad persons. Emulation makes us take steps to secure the good things in question, envy makes us take steps to stop our neighbour having them. Emulation must therefore tend to be felt by persons who believe themselves to deserve certain good things that they have not got, it being understood that no one aspires to things which appear impossible. It is accordingly felt by the young and by persons of lofty disposition. Also by those who possess such good things as are deserved by men held in honour-these are wealth, abundance of friends, public office, and the like; on the assumption that they ought to be good men, they are emulous to gain such goods because they ought, in their belief, to belong to men whose state of mind is good. Also by those whom all others think deserving. We also feel it about anything for which our ancestors, relatives, personal friends, race, or country are specially honoured, looking upon that thing as really our own, and therefore feeling that we deserve to have it. Further, since all good things that are highly honoured are objects of emulation, moral goodness in its various forms must be such an object, and also all those good things that are useful and serviceable to others: for men honour those who are morally good, and also those who do them service. So with those good things our possession of which can give enjoyment to our neighbours-wealth and beauty rather than health. We can see, too, what persons are the objects of the feeling. They are those who have these and similar things-those already mentioned, as courage, wisdom, public office. Holders of public office-generals, orators, and all who possess such powers-can do many people a good turn. Also those whom many people wish to be like; those who have many acquaintances or friends; those whom admire, or whom we ourselves admire; and those who have been praised and eulogized by poets or prose-writers. Persons of the contrary sort are objects of contempt: for the feeling and notion of contempt are opposite to those of emulation. Those who are such as to emulate or be emulated by others are inevitably disposed to be contemptuous of all such persons as are subject to those bad things which are contrary to the good things that are the objects of emulation: despising them for just that reason. Hence we often despise the fortunate, when luck comes to them without their having those good things which are held in honour.

This completes our discussion of the means by which the several emotions may be produced or dissipated, and upon which depend the persuasive arguments connected with the emotions.

Part 12

Let us now consider the various types of human character, in relation to the emotions and moral qualities, showing how they correspond to our various ages and fortunes. By emotions I mean anger, desire, and the like; these we have discussed already. By moral qualities I mean virtues and vices; these also have been discussed already, as well as the various things that various types of men tend to will and to do. By ages I mean youth, the prime of life, and old age. By fortune I mean birth, wealth, power, and their opposites-in fact, good fortune and ill fortune.

To begin with the Youthful type of character. Young men have strong passions, and tend to gratify them indiscriminately. Of the bodily desires, it is the sexual by which they are most swayed and in which they show absence of self-control. They are changeable and fickle in their desires, which are violent while they last, but quickly over: their impulses are keen but not deep-rooted, and are like sick people's attacks of hunger and thirst. They are hot-tempered, and quick-tempered, and apt to give way to their anger; bad temper often gets the better of them, for owing to their love of honour they cannot bear being slighted, and are indignant if they imagine themselves unfairly treated. While they love honour, they love victory still more; for youth is eager for superiority over others, and victory is one form of this. They love both more than they love money, which indeed they love very little, not having yet learnt what it means to be without it-this is the point of Pittacus' remark about Amphiaraus. They look at the good side rather than the bad, not having yet witnessed many instances of wickedness. They trust others readily, because they have not yet often been cheated. They are sanguine; nature warms their blood as though with excess of wine; and besides that, they have as yet met with few disappointments. Their lives are mainly spent not in memory but in expectation; for expectation refers to the future, memory to the past, and youth has a long future before it and a short past behind it: on the first day of one's life one has nothing at all to remember, and can only look forward. They are easily cheated, owing to the sanguine disposition just mentioned. Their hot tempers and hopeful dispositions make them more courageous than older men are; the hot temper prevents fear, and the hopeful disposition creates confidence; we cannot feel fear so long as we are feeling angry, and any expectation of good makes us confident. They are shy, accepting the rules of society in which they have been trained, and not yet believing in any other standard of honour. They have exalted notions, because they have not yet been humbled by life or learnt its necessary limitations; moreover, their hopeful disposition makes them think themselves equal to great things-and that means having exalted notions. They would always rather do noble deeds than useful ones: their lives are regulated more by moral feeling than by reasoning; and whereas reasoning leads us to choose what is useful, moral goodness leads us to choose what is noble. They are fonder of their friends, intimates, and companions than older men are, because they like spending their days in the company of others, and have not yet come to value either their friends or anything else by their usefulness to themselves. All their mistakes are in the direction of doing things excessively and vehemently. They disobey Chilon's precept by overdoing everything, they love too much and hate too much, and the same thing with everything else. They think they know everything, and are always quite sure about it; this, in fact, is why they overdo everything. If they do wrong to others, it is because they mean to insult them, not to do them actual harm. They are ready to pity others, because they think every one an honest man, or anyhow better than he is: they judge their neighbour by their own harmless natures, and so cannot think he deserves to be treated in that way. They are fond of fun and therefore witty, wit being well-bred insolence.

Part 13

Such, then is the character of the Young. The character of Elderly Men-men who are past their prime-may be said to be formed for the most part of elements that are the contrary of all these. They have lived many years; they have often been taken in, and often made mistakes; and life on the whole is a bad business. The result is that they are sure about nothing and under-do everything. They 'think', but they never 'know'; and because of their hesitation they always add a 'possibly'or a 'perhaps', putting everything this way and nothing positively. They are cynical; that is, they tend to put the worse construction on everything. Further, their experience makes them distrustful and therefore suspicious of evil. Consequently they neither love warmly nor hate bitterly, but following the hint of Bias they love as though they will some day hate and hate as though they will some day love. They are small-minded, because they have been humbled by life: their desires are set upon nothing more exalted or unusual than what will help them to keep alive. They are not generous, because money is one of the things they must have, and at the same time their experience has taught them how hard it is to get and how easy to lose. They are cowardly, and are always anticipating danger; unlike that of the young, who are warm-blooded, their temperament is chilly; old age has paved the way for cowardice; fear is, in fact, a form of chill. They love life; and all the more when their last day has come, because the object of all desire is something we have not got, and also because we desire most strongly that which we need most urgently. They are too fond of themselves; this is one form that small-mindedness takes. Because of this, they guide their lives too much by considerations of what is useful and too little by what is noble-for the useful is what is good for oneself, and the noble what is good absolutely. They are not shy, but shameless rather; caring less for what is noble than for what is useful, they feel contempt for what people may think of them. They lack confidence in the future; partly through experience-for most things go wrong, or anyhow turn out worse than one expects; and partly because of their cowardice. They live by memory rather than by hope; for what is left to them of life is but little as compared with the long past; and hope is of the future, memory of the past. This, again, is the cause of their loquacity; they are continually talking of the past, because they enjoy remembering it. Their fits of anger are sudden but feeble. Their sensual passions have either altogether gone or have lost their vigour: consequently they do not feel their passions much, and their actions are inspired less by what they do feel than by the love of gain. Hence men at this time of life are often supposed to have a self-controlled character; the fact is that their passions have slackened, and they are slaves to the love of gain. They guide their lives by reasoning more than by moral feeling; reasoning being directed to utility and moral feeling to moral goodness. If they wrong others, they mean to injure them, not to insult them. Old men may feel pity, as well as young men, but not for the same reason. Young men feel it out of kindness; old men out of weakness, imagining that anything that befalls any one else might easily happen to them, which, as we saw, is a thought that excites pity. Hence they are querulous, and not disposed to jesting or laughter-the love of laughter being the very opposite of querulousness.

Such are the characters of Young Men and Elderly Men. People always think well of speeches adapted to, and reflecting, their own character: and we can now see how to compose our speeches so as to adapt both them and ourselves to our audiences.

Part 14

As for Men in their Prime, clearly we shall find that they have a character between that of the young and that of the old, free from the extremes of either. They have neither that excess of confidence which amounts to rashness, nor too much timidity, but the right amount of each. They neither trust everybody nor distrust everybody, but judge people correctly. Their lives will be guided not by the sole consideration either of what is noble or of what is useful, but by both; neither by parsimony nor by prodigality, but by what is fit and proper. So, too, in regard to anger and desire; they will be brave as well as temperate, and temperate as well as brave; these virtues are divided between the young and the old; the young are brave but intemperate, the old temperate but cowardly. To put it generally, all the valuable qualities that youth and age divide between them are united in the prime of life, while all their excesses or defects are replaced by moderation and fitness. The body is in its prime from thirty to five-and-thirty; the mind about forty-nine.

Part 15

So much for the types of character that distinguish youth, old age, and the prime of life. We will now turn to those Gifts of Fortune by which human character is affected. First let us consider Good Birth. Its effect on character is to make those who have it more ambitious; it is the way of all men who have something to start with to add to the pile, and good birth implies ancestral distinction. The well-born man will look down even on those who are as good as his own ancestors, because any far-off distinction is greater than the same thing close to us, and better to boast about. Being well-born, which means coming of a fine stock, must be distinguished from nobility, which means being true to the family nature-a quality not usually found in the well-born, most of whom are poor creatures. In the generations of men as in the fruits of the earth, there is a varying yield; now and then, where the stock is good, exceptional men are produced for a while, and then decadence sets in. A clever stock will degenerate towards the insane type of character, like the descendants of Alcibiades or of the elder Dionysius; a steady stock towards the fatuous and torpid type, like the descendants of Cimon, Pericles, and Socrates.

Part 16

The type of character produced by Wealth lies on the surface for all to see. Wealthy men are insolent and arrogant; their possession of wealth affects their understanding; they feel as if they had every good thing that exists; wealth becomes a sort of standard of value for everything else, and therefore they imagine there is nothing it cannot buy. They are luxurious and ostentatious;

luxurious, because of the luxury in which they live and the prosperity which they display; ostentatious and vulgar, because, like other people's, their minds are regularly occupied with the object of their love and admiration, and also because they think that other people's idea of happiness is the same as their own. It is indeed quite natural that they should be affected thus; for if you have money, there are always plenty of people who come begging from you. Hence the saying of Simonides about wise men and rich men, in answer to Hiero's wife, who asked him whether it was better to grow rich or wise. "Why, rich," he said; "for I see the wise men spending their days at the rich men's doors." Rich men also consider themselves worthy to hold public office; for they consider they already have the things that give a claim to office. In a word, the type of character produced by wealth is that of a prosperous fool. There is indeed one difference between the type of the newly-enriched and those who have long been rich: the newly-enriched have all the bad qualities mentioned in an exaggerated and worse form -- to be newly-enriched means, so to speak, no education in riches. The wrongs they do others are not meant to injure their victims, but spring from insolence or self-indulgence, e.g. those that end in assault or in adultery.

Part 17

As to Power: here too it may fairly be said that the type of character it produces is mostly obvious enough. Some elements in this type it shares with the wealthy type, others are better. Those in power are more ambitious and more manly in character than the wealthy, because they aspire to do the great deeds that their power permits them to do. Responsibility makes them more serious: they have to keep paying attention to the duties their position involves. They are dignified rather than arrogant, for the respect in which they are held inspires them with dignity and therefore with moderation -- dignity being a mild and becoming form of arrogance. If they wrong others, they wrong them not on a small but on a great scale.

Good fortune in certain of its branches produces the types of character belonging to the conditions just described, since these conditions are in fact more or less the kinds of good fortune that are regarded as most important. It may be added that good fortune leads us to gain all we can in the way of family happiness and bodily advantages. It does indeed make men more supercilious and more reckless; but there is one excellent quality that goes with it -- piety, and respect for the divine power, in which they believe because of events which are really the result of chance.

This account of the types of character that correspond to differences of age or fortune may end here; for to arrive at the opposite types to those described, namely, those of the poor, the unfortunate, and the powerless, we have only to ask what the opposite qualities are.

Part 18

The use of persuasive speech is to lead to decisions. (When we know a thing, and have decided about it, there is no further use in speaking about it.) This is so even if one is addressing a single person and urging him to do or not to do something, as when we scold a man for his conduct or try to change his views: the single person is as much your "judge" as if he were one of many; we may say, without qualification, that any one is your judge whom you have to persuade. Nor does it matter whether we are arguing against an actual opponent or against a mere proposition; in the latter case we still have to use speech and overthrow the opposing arguments, and we attack these as we should attack an actual opponent. Our principle holds good of ceremonial speeches also; the "onlookers" for whom such a speech is put together are treated as the judges of it. Broadly speaking, however, the only sort of person who can strictly be called a judge is the man who decides the issue in some matter of public controversy; that is, in law suits and in political debates, in both of which there are issues to be decided. In the section on political oratory an account has already been given of the types of character that mark the different constitutions.

The manner and means of investing speeches with moral character may now be regarded as fully set forth.

Each of the main divisions of oratory has, we have seen, its own distinct purpose. With regard to each division, we have noted the accepted views and propositions upon which we may base our arguments -- for political, for ceremonial, and for forensic speaking. We have further determined completely by what means speeches may be invested with the required moral character. We are now to proceed to discuss the arguments common to all oratory. All orators, besides their special lines of argument, are bound to use, for instance, the topic of the Possible and Impossible; and to try to show that a thing has happened, or will happen in future. Again, the topic of Size is common to all oratory; all of us have to argue that things are bigger or smaller than they seem, whether we are making political speeches, speeches of eulogy or attack, or prosecuting or defending in the law-courts. Having analysed these subjects, we will try to say what we can about the general principles of arguing by "enthymeme" and "example," by the addition of which we may hope to complete the project with which we set out. Of the above-mentioned general lines of argument, that concerned with Amplification is -- as has been already said -- most appropriate to ceremonial speeches; that concerned with the Past, to forensic speeches, where the required decision is always about the past; that concerned with Possibility and the Future, to political speeches.

Part 19

Let us first speak of the Possible and Impossible. It may plausibly be argued: That if it is possible for one of a pair of contraries to be or happen, then it is possible for the other: e.g. if a man can be cured, he can also fall ill; for any two contraries are equally possible, in so far as they are contraries. That if of two similar things one is possible, so is the other. That if the harder of two things is possible, so is the easier. That if a thing can come into existence in a good and beautiful form, then it can come into existence generally; thus a house can exist more easily than a beautiful house. That if the beginning of a thing can occur, so can the end; for nothing impossible occurs or begins to occur; thus the commensurability of the diagonal of a square with its side neither occurs nor can begin to occur. That if the end is possible, so is the beginning; for all things that occur have a beginning. That if that which is posterior in essence or in order of generation can come into being, so can that which is prior: thus if a man can come into being, so can a boy, since the boy comes first in order of generation; and if a boy can, so can a man, for the man also is first. That those things are possible of which the love or desire is natural; for no one, as a rule, loves or desires impossibilities. That things which are the object of any kind of science or art are possible and exist or come into existence. That anything is possible the first step in whose production depends on men or things which we can compel or persuade to produce it, by our greater strength, our control of them, or our friendship with them. That where the parts are possible, the whole is possible; and where the whole is possible, the parts are usually possible. For if the slit in front, the toe-piece, and the upper leather can be made, then shoes can be made; and if shoes, then also the front slit and toe-piece. That if a whole genus is a thing that can occur, so can the species; and if the species can occur, so can the genus: thus, if a sailing vessel can be made, so also can a trireme; and if a trireme, then a sailing vessel also. That if one of two things whose existence depends on each other is possible, so is the other; for instance, if "double," then "half," and if "half," then "double." That if a thing can be produced without art or preparation, it can be produced still more certainly by the careful application of art to it. Hence Agathon has said:

To some things we by art must needs attain,
Others by destiny or luck we gain.

That if anything is possible to inferior, weaker, and stupider people, it is more so for their opposites; thus Isocrates said that it would be a strange thing if he could not discover a thing that Euthynus had found out. As for Impossibility, we can clearly get what we want by taking the contraries of the arguments stated above.

Questions of Past Fact may be looked at in the following ways: First, that if the less likely of two things has occurred, the more likely must have occurred also. That if one thing that usually follows another has happened, then that other thing has happened; that, for instance, if a man has forgotten a thing, he has also once learnt it. That if a man had the power and the wish to do a thing, he has done it; for every one does do whatever he intends to do whenever he can do it, there being nothing to stop him. That, further, he has done the thing in question either if he intended it and nothing external prevented him; or if he had the power to do it and was angry at the time; or if he had the power to do it and his heart was set upon it -- for people as a rule do what they long to do, if they can; bad people through lack of self-control; good people, because their hearts are set upon good things. Again, that if a thing was "going to happen," it has happened; if a man was "going to do something," he has done it, for it is likely that the intention was carried out. That if one thing has happened which naturally happens before another or with a view to it, the other has happened; for instance, if it has lightened, it has also thundered; and if an action has been attempted, it has been done. That if one thing has happened which naturally happens after another, or with a view to which that other happens, then that other (that which happens first, or happens with a view to this thing) has also happened; thus, if it has thundered it has lightened, and if an action has been done it has been attempted. Of all these sequences some are inevitable and some merely usual. The arguments for the non-occurrence of anything can obviously be found by considering the opposites of those that have been mentioned.

How questions of Future Fact should be argued is clear from the same considerations: That a thing will be done if there is both the power and the wish to do it; or if along with the power to do it there is a craving for the result, or anger, or calculation, prompting it. That the thing will be done, in these cases, if the man is actually setting about it, or even if he means to do it later -- for usually what we mean to do happens rather than what we do not mean to do. That a thing will happen if another thing which naturally happens before it has already happened; thus, if it is clouding over, it is likely to rain. That if the means to an end have occurred, then the end is likely to occur; thus, if there is a foundation, there will be a house.

For arguments about the Greatness and Smallness of things, the greater and the lesser, and generally great things and small, what we have already said will show the line to take. In discussing deliberative oratory we have spoken about the relative greatness of various goods, and about the greater and lesser in general. Since therefore in each type oratory the object under discussion is some kind of good -- whether it is utility, nobleness, or justice -- it is clear that every orator must obtain the materials of amplification through these channels. To go further than this, and try to establish abstract laws of greatness and superiority, is to argue without an object; in practical life, particular facts count more than generalizations.

Enough has now been said about these questions of possibility and the reverse, of past or future fact, and of the relative greatness or smallness of things.

Part 20

The special forms of oratorical argument having now been discussed, we have next to treat of those which are common to all kinds of oratory. These are of two main kinds, "Example" and "Enthymeme"; for the "Maxim" is part of an enthymeme.

We will first treat of argument by Example, for it has the nature of induction, which is the foundation of reasoning. This form of argument has two varieties; one consisting in the mention of actual past facts, the other in the invention of facts by the speaker. Of the latter, again, there are two varieties, the illustrative parallel and the fable (e.g. the fables of Aesop, those from Libya). As an instance of the mention of actual facts, take the following. The speaker may argue thus: "We must prepare for war against the king of Persia and not let him subdue Egypt. For Darius of old did not cross the Aegean until he had seized Egypt; but once he had seized it, he did cross. And Xerxes, again, did not attack us until he had seized Egypt; but once he had seized it, he did cross. If therefore the present king seizes Egypt, he also will cross, and therefore we must not let him."

The illustrative parallel is the sort of argument Socrates used: e.g. "Public officials ought not to be selected by lot. That is like using the lot to select athletes, instead of choosing those who are fit for the contest; or using the lot to select a steersman from among a ship's crew, as if we ought to take the man on whom the lot falls, and not the man who knows most about it."

Instances of the fable are that of Stesichorus about Phalaris, and that of Aesop in defence of the popular leader. When the people of Himera had made Phalaris military dictator, and were going to give him a bodyguard, Stesichorus wound up a long talk by telling them the fable of the horse who had a field all to himself. Presently there came a stag and began to spoil his pasturage. The horse, wishing to revenge himself on the stag, asked a man if he could help him to do so. The man said, "Yes, if you will let me bridle you and get on to your back with javelins in my hand." The horse agreed, and the man mounted; but instead of getting his revenge on the stag, the horse found himself the slave of the man. "You too," said Stesichorus, "take care lest your desire for revenge on your enemies, you meet the same fate as the horse. By making Phalaris military dictator, you have already let yourselves be bridled. If you let him get on to your backs by giving him a bodyguard, from that moment you will be his slaves."

Aesop, defending before the assembly at Samos a poular leader who was being tried for his life, told this story: A fox, in crossing a river, was swept into a hole in the rocks; and, not being able to get out, suffered miseries for a long time through the swarms of fleas that fastened on her. A hedgehog, while roaming around, noticed the fox; and feeling sorry for her asked if he might remove the fleas. But the fox declined the offer; and when the hedgehog asked why, she replied, "These fleas are by this time full of me and not sucking much blood; if you take them away, others will come with fresh appetites and drink up all the blood I have left." "So, men of Samos," said Aesop, "my client will do you no further harm; he is wealthy already. But if you put him to death, others will come along who are not rich, and their peculations will empty your treasury completely."

Fables are suitable for addresses to popular assemblies; and they have one advantage -- they are comparatively easy to invent, whereas it is hard to find parallels among actual past events. You will in fact frame them just as you frame illustrative parallels: all you require is the power of thinking out your analogy, a power developed by intellectual training. But while it is easier to supply parallels by inventing fables, it is more valuable for the political speaker to supply them by quoting what has actually happened, since in most respects the future will be like what the past has been.

Where we are unable to argue by Enthymeme, we must try to demonstrate our point by this method of Example, and to convince our hearers thereby. If we can argue by Enthymeme, we should use our Examples as subsequent supplementary evidence. They should not precede the Enthymemes: that will give the argument an inductive air, which only rarely suits the conditions of speech-making. If they follow the enthymemes, they have the effect of witnesses giving evidence, and this alway tells. For the same reason, if you put your examples first you must give a large number of them; if you put them last, a single one is sufficient; even a single witness will serve if he is a good one. It has now been stated how many varieties of argument by Example there are, and how and when they are to be employed.

Part 21

We now turn to the use of Maxims, in order to see upon what subjects and occasions, and for what kind of speaker, they will appropriately form part of a speech. This will appear most clearly when we have defined a maxim. It is a statement; not a particular fact, such as the character of Iphicrates, but of a general kind; nor is it about any and every subject -- e.g. "straight is the contrary of curved" is not a maxim -- but only about questions of practical conduct, courses of conduct to be chosen or avoided. Now an Enthymeme is a syllogism dealing with such practical subjects. It is therefore roughly true that the premisses or conclusions of Enthymemes, considered apart from the rest of the argument, are Maxims: e.g.

Never should any man whose wits are sound
Have his sons taught more wisdom than their fellows.

Here we have a Maxim; add the reason or explanation, and the whole thing is an Enthymeme; thus --

It makes them idle; and therewith they earn
Ill-will and jealousy throughout the city.

Again,

There is no man in all things prosperous,

and

There is no man among us all is free,

are maxims; but the latter, taken with what follows it, is an Enthymeme --

For all are slaves of money or of chance.

From this definition of a maxim it follows that there are four kinds of maxims. In the first Place, the maxim may or may not have a supplement. Proof is needed where the statement is paradoxical or disputable; no supplement is wanted where the statement contains nothing paradoxical, either because the view expressed is already a known truth, e.g.

Chiefest of blessings is health for a man, as it seemeth to me,

this being the general opinion: or because, as soon as the view is stated, it is clear at a glance, e.g.

No love is true save that which loves for ever.

Of the Maxims that do have a supplement attached, some are part of an Enthymeme, e.g.

Never should any man whose wits are sound, &c.

Others have the essential character of Enthymemes, but are not stated as parts of Enthymemes; these latter are reckoned the best; they are those in which the reason for the view expressed is simply implied, e.g.

O mortal man, nurse not immortal wrath.

To say "it is not right to nurse immortal wrath" is a maxim; the added words "mortal man" give the reason. Similarly, with the words

Mortal creatures ought to cherish mortal, not immortal thoughts.

What has been said has shown us how many kinds of Maxims there are, and to what subjects the various kinds are appropriate. They must not be given without supplement if they express disputed or paradoxical views: we must, in that case, either put the supplement first and make a maxim of the conclusion, e.g. you might say, "For my part, since both unpopularity and idleness are undesirable, I hold that it is better not to be educated"; or you may say this first, and then add the previous clause. Where a statement, without being paradoxical, is not obviously true, the reason should be added as concisely as possible. In such cases both laconic and enigmatic sayings are suitable: thus one might say what Stesichorus said to the Locrians, "Insolence is better avoided, lest the cicadas chirp on the ground."

The use of Maxims is appropriate only to elderly men, and in handling subjects in which the speaker is experienced. For a young man to use them is -- like telling stories -- unbecoming; to use them in handling things in which one has no experience is silly and ill-bred: a fact sufficiently proved by the special fondness of country fellows for striking out maxims, and their readiness to air them.

To declare a thing to be universally true when it is not is most appropriate when working up feelings of horror and indignation in our hearers; especially by way of preface, or after the facts have been proved. Even hackneyed and commonplace maxims are to be used, if they suit one's purpose: just because they are commonplace, every one seems to agree with them, and therefore they are taken for truth. Thus, any one who is calling on his men to risk an engagement without obtaining favourable omens may quote

One omen of all is hest, that we fight for our fatherland.

Or, if he is calling on them to attack a stronger force-

The War-God showeth no favour.

Or, if he is urging people to destroy the innocent children of their enemies --

Fool, who slayeth the father and leaveth his sons to avenge him.

Some proverbs are also maxims, e.g. the proverb "An Attic neighbour." You are not to avoid uttering maxims that contradict such sayings as have become public property (I mean such sayings as "know thyself" and "nothing in excess") if doing so will raise your hearers' opinion of your character, or convey an effect of strong emotion -- e.g. an angry speaker might well say, "It is not true that we ought to know ourselves: anyhow, if this man had known himself, he would never have thought himself fit for an army command." It will raise people's opinion of our character to say, for instance, "We ought not to follow the saying that bids us treat our friends as future enemies: much better to treat our enemies as future friends." The moral purpose should be implied partly by the very wording of our maxim. Failing this, we should add our reason: e.g. having said "We should treat our friends, not as the saying advises, but as if they were going to be our friends always," we should add "for the other behaviour is that of a traitor": or we might put it, I disapprove of that saying. A true friend will treat his friend as if he were going to be his friend for ever"; and again, "Nor do I approve of the saying "nothing in excess": we are bound to hate bad men excessively."

One great advantage of Maxims to a speaker is due to the want of intelligence in his hearers, who love to hear him succeed in expressing as a universal truth the opinions which they hold themselves about particular cases. I will explain what I mean by this, indicating at the same time how we are to hunt down the maxims required. The maxim, as has been already said, a general statement and people love to hear stated in general terms what they already believe in some particular connexion: e.g. if a man happens to have bad neighbours or bad children, he will agree with any one who tells him, "Nothing is more annoying than having neighbours," or, "Nothing is more foolish than to be the parent of children." The orator has therefore to guess the subjects on which his hearers really hold views already, and what those views are, and then must express, as general truths, these same views on these same subjects. This is one advantage of using maxims. There is another which is more important -- it invests a speech with moral character. There is moral character in every speech in which the moral purpose is conspicuous: and maxims always produce this effect, because the utterance of them amounts to a general declaration of moral principles: so that, if the maxims are sound, they display the speaker as a man of sound moral character. So much for the Maxim -- its nature, varieties, proper use, and advantages.

Part 22

We now come to the Enthymemes, and will begin the subject with some general consideration of the proper way of looking for them, and then proceed to what is a distinct question, the lines of argument to be embodied in them. It has already been pointed out that the Enthymeme is a syllogism, and in what sense it is so. We have also noted the differences between it and the syllogism of dialectic. Thus we must not carry its reasoning too far back, or the length of our argument will cause obscurity: nor must we put in all the steps that lead to our conclusion, or we shall waste words in saying what is manifest. It is this simplicity that makes the uneducated more effective than the educated when addressing popular audiences -- makes them, as the poets tell us, "charm the crowd's ears more finely." Educated men lay down broad general principles; uneducated men argue from common knowledge and draw obvious conclusions. We must not, therefore, start from any and every accepted opinion, but only from those we have defined -- those accepted by our judges or by those whose authority they recognize: and there must, moreover, be no doubt in the minds of most, if not all, of our judges that the opinions put forward really are of this sort. We should also base our arguments upon probabilities as well as upon certainties.

The first thing we have to remember is this. Whether our argument concerns public affairs or some other subject, we must know some, if not all, of the facts about the subject on which we are to speak and argue. Otherwise we can have no materials out of which to construct arguments. I mean, for instance, how could we advise the Athenians whether they should go to war or not, if we did not know their strength, whether it was naval or military or both, and how great it is; what their revenues amount to; who their friends and enemies are; what wars, too, they have waged, and with what success; and so on? Or how could we eulogize them if we knew nothing about the sea-fight at Salamis, or the battle of Marathon, or what they did for the Heracleidae, or any other facts like that? All eulogy is based upon the noble deeds -- real or imaginary -- that stand to the credit of those eulogized. On the same principle, invectives are based on facts of the opposite kind: the orator looks to see what base deeds -- real or imaginary -- stand to the discredit of those he is attacking, such as treachery to the cause of Hellenic freedom, or the enslavement of their gallant allies against the barbarians (Aegina, Potidaea, &c.), or any other misdeeds of this kind that are recorded against them. So, too, in a court of law: whether we are prosecuting or defending, we must pay attention to the existing facts of the case. It makes no difference whether the subject is the Lacedaemonians or the Athenians, a man or a god; we must do the same thing. Suppose it to be Achilles whom we are to advise, to praise or blame, to accuse or defend; here too we must take the facts, real or imaginary; these must be our material, whether we are to praise or blame him for the noble or base deeds he has done, to accuse or defend him for his just or unjust treatment of others, or to advise him about what is or is not to his interest. The same thing applies to any subject whatever. Thus, in handling the question whether justice is or is not a good, we must start with the real facts about justice and goodness. We see, then, that this is the only way in which any one ever proves anything, whether his arguments are strictly cogent or not: not all facts can form his basis, but only those that bear on the matter in hand: nor, plainly, can proof be effected otherwise by means of the speech. Consequently, as appears in the Topics, we must first of all have by us a selection of arguments about questions that may arise and are suitable for us to handle; and then we must try to think out arguments of the same type for special needs as they emerge; not vaguely and indefinitely, but by keeping our eyes on the actual facts of the subject we have to speak on, and gathering in as many of them as we can that bear closely upon it: for the more actual facts we have at our command, the more easily we prove our case; and the more closely they bear on the subject, the more they will seem to belong to that speech only instead of being commonplaces. By "commonplaces" I mean, for example, eulogy of Achilles because he is a human being or a demi-god, or because he joined the expedition against Troy: these things are true of many others, so that this kind of eulogy applies no better to Achilles than to Diomede. The special facts here needed are those that are true of Achilles alone; such facts as that he slew Hector, the bravest of the Trojans, and Cycnus the invulnerable, who prevented all the Greeks from landing, and again that he was the youngest man who joined the expedition, and was not bound by oath to join it, and so on.

Here, again, we have our first principle of selection of Enthymemes -- that which refers to the lines of argument selected. We will now consider the various elementary classes of enthymemes. (By an "elementary class" of enthymeme I mean the same thing as a "line of argument.") We will begin, as we must begin, by observing that there are two kinds of enthymemes. One kind proves some affirmative or negative proposition; the other kind disproves one. The difference between the two kinds is the same as that between syllogistic proof and disproof in dialectic. The demonstrative enthymeme is formed by the conjunction of compatible propositions; the refutative, by the conjunction of incompatible propositions.

We may now be said to have in our hands the lines of argument for the various special subjects that it is useful or necessary to handle, having selected the propositions suitable in various cases. We have, in fact, already ascertained the lines of argument applicable to enthymemes about good and evil, the noble and the base, justice and injustice, and also to those about types of character, emotions, and moral qualities. Let us now lay hold of certain facts about the whole subject, considered from a different and more general point of view. In the course of our discussion we will take note of the distinction between lines of proof and lines of disproof: and also of those lines of argument used in what seems to be enthymemes, but are not, since they do not represent valid syllogisms. Having made all this clear, we will proceed to classify Objections and Refutations, showing how they can be brought to bear upon enthymemes.

Part 23

1. One line of positive proof is based upon consideration of the opposite of the thing in question. Observe whether that opposite has the opposite quality. If it has not, you refute the original proposition; if it has, you establish it. E.g. "Temperance is beneficial; for licentiousness is hurtful." Or, as in the Messenian speech, "If war is the cause of our present troubles, peace is what we need to put things right again." Or --

For if not even evil-doers should
Anger us if they meant not what they did,
Then can we owe no gratitude to such
As were constrained to do the good they did us.

Or --

Since in this world liars may win belief,
Be sure of the opposite likewise-that this world
Hears many a true word and believes it not.

2. Another line of proof is got by considering some modification of the key-word, and arguing

that what can or cannot be said of the one, can or cannot be said of the other: e.g. "just" does not always mean "beneficial," or "justly" would always mean "beneficially," whereas it is not desirable to be justly put to death.

3. Another line of proof is based upon correlative ideas. If it is true that one man gave noble or just treatment to another, you argue that the other must have received noble or just treatment; or that where it is right to command obedience, it must have been right to obey the command. Thus Diomedon, the tax-farmer, said of the taxes: "If it is no disgrace for you to sell them, it is no disgrace for us to buy them." Further, if "well" or "justly" is true of the person to whom a thing is done, you argue that it is true of the doer. But it is possible to draw a false conclusion here. It may be just that A should be treated in a certain way, and yet not just that he should be so treated by B. Hence you must ask yourself two distinct questions: (1) Is it right that A should be thus treated? (2) Is it right that B should thus treat him? and apply your results properly, according as your answers are Yes or No. Sometimes in such a case the two answers differ: you may quite easily have a position like that in the Alcmaeon of Theodectes:

And was there none to loathe thy mother's crime?

to which question Alcmaeon in reply says,

Why, there are two things to examine here.

And when Alphesiboea asks what he means, he rejoins:

They judged her fit to die, not me to slay her.

Again there is the lawsuit about Demosthenes and the men who killed Nicanor; as they were judged to have killed him justly, it was thought that he was killed justly. And in the case of the man who was killed at Thebes, the judges were requested to decide whether it was unjust that he should be killed, since if it was not, it was argued that it could not have been unjust to kill him.

4. Another line of proof is the a fortiori. Thus it may be argued that if even the gods are not omniscient, certainly human beings are not. The principle here is that, if a quality does not in fact exist where it is more likely to exist, it clearly does not exist where it is less likely. Again, the argument that a man who strikes his father also strikes his neighbours follows from the principle that, if the less likely thing is true, the more likely thing is true also; for a man is less likely to strike his father than to strike his neighbours. The argument, then, may run thus. Or it may be urged that, if a thing is not true where it is more likely, it is not true where it is less likely; or that, if it is true where it is less likely, it is true where it is more likely: according as we have to show that a thing is or is not true. This argument might also be used in a case of parity, as in the lines:

Thou hast pity for thy sire, who has lost his sons:
Hast none for Oeneus, whose brave son is dead?

And, again, "if Theseus did no wrong, neither did Paris"; or "the sons of Tyndareus did no wrong, neither did Paris"; or "if Hector did well to slay Patroclus, Paris did well to slay

Achilles." And "if other followers of an art are not bad men, neither are philosophers." And "if generals are not bad men because it often happens that they are condemned to death, neither are sophists." And the remark that "if each individual among you ought to think of his own city's reputation, you ought all to think of the reputation of Greece as a whole."

5. Another line of argument is based on considerations of time. Thus Iphicrates, in the case against Harmodius, said, "if before doing the deed I had bargained that, if I did it, I should have a statue, you would have given me one. Will you not give me one now that I have done the deed? You must not make promises when you are expecting a thing to be done for you, and refuse to fulfil them when the thing has been done." And, again, to induce the Thebans to let Philip pass through their territory into Attica, it was argued that "if he had insisted on this before he helped them against the Phocians, they would have promised to do it. It is monstrous, therefore, that just because he threw away his advantage then, and trusted their honour, they should not let him pass through now."

6. Another line is to apply to the other speaker what he has said against yourself. It is an excellent turn to give to a debate, as may be seen in the Teucer. It was employed by Iphicrates in his reply to Aristophon. "Would you," he asked, "take a bribe to betray the fleet?" "No," said Aristophon; and Iphicrates replied, "Very good: if you, who are Aristophon, would not betray the fleet, would I, who am Iphicrates?" Only, it must be recognized beforehand that the other man is more likely than you are to commit the crime in question. Otherwise you will make yourself ridiculous; it is Aristeides who is prosecuting, you cannot say that sort of thing to him. The purpose is to discredit the prosecutor, who as a rule would have it appear that his character is better than that of the defendant, a pretension which it is desirable to upset. But the use of such an argument is in all cases ridiculous if you are attacking others for what you do or would do yourself, or are urging others to do what you neither do nor would do yourself.

7. Another line of proof is secured by defining your terms. Thus, "What is the supernatural? Surely it is either a god or the work of a god. Well, any one who believes that the work of a god exists, cannot help also believing that gods exist." Or take the argument of Iphicrates, "Goodness is true nobility; neither Harmodius nor Aristogeiton had any nobility before they did a noble deed." He also argued that he himself was more akin to Harmodius and Aristogeiton than his opponent was. "At any rate, my deeds are more akin to those of Harmodius and Aristogeiton than yours are." Another example may be found in the Alexander. "Every one will agree that by incontinent people we mean those who are not satisfied with the enjoyment of one love." A further example is to be found in the reason given by Socrates for not going to the court of Archelaus. He said that "one is insulted by being unable to requite benefits, as well as by being unable to requite injuries." All the persons mentioned define their term and get at its essential meaning, and then use the result when reasoning on the point at issue.

8. Another line of argument is founded upon the various senses of a word. Such a word is "rightly," as has been explained in the Topics.

9. Another line is based upon logical division. Thus, "All men do wrong from one of three motives, A, B, or C: in my case A and B are out of the question, and even the accusers do not allege C."

10. Another line is based upon induction. Thus from the case of the woman of Peparethus it might be argued that women everywhere can settle correctly the facts about their children. Another example of this occurred at Athens in the case between the orator Mantias and his son, when the boy's mother revealed the true facts: and yet another at Thebes, in the case between Ismenias and Stilbon, when Dodonis proved that it was Ismenias who was the father of her son Thettaliscus, and he was in consequence always regarded as being so. A further instance of induction may be taken from the Law of Theodectes: "If we do not hand over our horses to the care of men who have mishandled other people's horses, nor ships to those who have wrecked other people's ships, and if this is true of everything else alike, then men who have failed to secure other people's safety are not to be employed to secure our own." Another instance is the argument of Alcidamas: "Every one honours the wise." Thus the Parians have honoured Archilochus, in spite of his bitter tongue; the Chians Homer, though he was not their countryman; the Mytilenaeans Sappho, though she was a woman; the Lacedaemonians actually made Chilon a member of their senate, though they are the least literary of men; the Italian Greeks honoured Pythagoras; the inhabitants of Lampsacus gave public burial to Anaxagoras, though he was an alien, and honour him even to this day. (It may be argued that peoples for whom philosophers legislate are always prosperous) on the ground that the Athenians became prosperous under Solon's laws and the Lacedaemonians under those of Lycurgus, while at Thebes no sooner did the leading men become philosophers than the country began to prosper.

11. Another line of argument is founded upon some decision already pronounced, whether on the same subject or on one like it or contrary to it. Such a proof is most effective if every one has always decided thus; but if not every one, then at any rate most people; or if all, or most, wise or good men have thus decided, or the actual judges of the present question, or those whose authority they accept, or any one whose decision they cannot gainsay because he has complete control over them, or those whom it is not seemly to gainsay, as the gods, or one's father, or one's teachers. Thus Autocles said, when attacking Mixidemides, that it was a strange thing that the Dread Goddesses could without loss of dignity submit to the judgement of the Areopagus, and yet Mixidemides could not. Or as Sappho said, "Death is an evil thing; the gods have so judged it, or they would die." Or again as Aristippus said in reply to Plato when he spoke somewhat too dogmatically, as Aristippus thought: "Well, anyhow, our friend," meaning Socrates, "never spoke like that." And Hegesippus, having previously consulted Zeus at Olympia, asked Apollo at Delphi "whether his opinion was the same as his father's," implying that it would be shameful for him to contradict his father. Thus too Isocrates argued that Helen must have been a good woman, because Theseus decided that she was; and Paris a good man, because the goddesses chose him before all others; and Evagoras also, says Isocrates, was good, since when Conon met with his misfortune he betook himself to Evagoras without trying any one else on the way.

12. Another line of argument consists in taking separately the parts of a subject. Such is that given in the Topics: "What sort of motion is the soul? for it must be this or that." The Socrates of Theodectes provides an example: "What temple has he profaned? What gods recognized by the state has he not honoured?"

13. Since it happens that any given thing usually has both good and bad consequences, another line of argument consists in using those consequences as a reason for urging that a thing should

or should not be done, for prosecuting or defending any one, for eulogy or censure. E.g. education leads both to unpopularity, which is bad, and to wisdom, which is good. Hence you either argue, "It is therefore not well to be educated, since it is not well to be unpopular": or you answer, "No, it is well to be educated, since it is well to be wise." The Art of Rhetoric of Callippus is made up of this line of argument, with the addition of those of Possibility and the others of that kind already described.

14. Another line of argument is used when we have to urge or discourage a course of action that may be done in either of two opposite ways, and have to apply the method just mentioned to both. The difference between this one and the last is that, whereas in the last any two things are contrasted, here the things contrasted are opposites. For instance, the priestess enjoined upon her son not to take to public speaking: "For," she said, "if you say what is right, men will hate you; if you say what is wrong, the gods will hate you." The reply might be, "On the contrary, you ought to take to public speaking: for if you say what is right the gods will love you; if you say what is wrong, men will love you." This amounts to the proverbial "buying the marsh with the salt." It is just this situation, viz. when each of two opposites has both a good and a bad consequence opposite respectively to each other, that has been termed divarication.

15. Another line of argument is this: The things people approve of openly are not those which they approve of secretly: openly, their chief praise is given to justice and nobleness; but in their hearts they prefer their own advantage. Try, in face of this, to establish the point of view which your opponent has not adopted. This is the most effective of the forms of argument that contradict common opinion.

16. Another line is that of rational correspondence. E.g. Iphicrates, when they were trying to compel his son, a youth under the prescribed age, to perform one of the state duties because he was tall, said "If you count tall boys men, you will next be voting short men boys." [1399b] And Theodectes in his Law said, "You make citizens of such mercenaries as Strabax and Charidemus, as a reward of their merits; will you not make exiles of such citizens as those who have done irreparable harm among the mercenaries?"

17. Another line is the argument that if two results are the same their antecedents are also the same. For instance, it was a saying of Xenophanes that to assert that the gods had birth is as impious as to say that they die; the consequence of both statements is that there is a time when the gods do not exist. This line of proof assumes generally that the result of any given thing is always the same: e.g. "you are going to decide not about Isocrates, but about the value of the whole profession of philosophy." Or, "to give earth and water" means slavery; or, "to share in the Common Peace" means obeying orders. We are to make either such assumptions or their opposite, as suits us best.

18. Another line of argument is based on the fact that men do not always make the same choice on a later as on an earlier occasion, but reverse their previous choice. E.g. the following enthymeme: "When we were exiles, we fought in order to return; now we have returned, it would be strange to choose exile in order not to have to fight." one occasion, that is, they chose to be true to their homes at the cost of fighting, and on the other to avoid fighting at the cost of deserting their homes.

19. Another line of argument is the assertion that some possible motive for an event or state of things is the real one: e.g. that a gift was given in order to cause pain by its withdrawal. This notion underlies the lines:

God gives to many great prosperity,
Not of good God towards them, but to make
The ruin of them more conspicuous.

Or take the passage from the Meleager of Antiphon:

To slay no boar, but to be witnesses
Of Meleager's prowess unto Greece.

Or the argument in the Ajax of Theodectes, that Diomede chose out Odysseus not to do him honour, but in order that his companion might be a lesser man than himself -- such a motive for doing so is quite possible.

20. Another line of argument is common to forensic and deliberative oratory, namely, to consider inducements and deterrents, and the motives people have for doing or avoiding the actions in question. These are the conditions which make us bound to act if they are for us, and to refrain from action if they are against us: that is, we are bound to act if the action is possible, easy, and useful to ourselves or our friends or hurtful to our enemies; this is true even if the action entails loss, provided the loss is outweighed by the solid advantage. A speaker will urge action by pointing to such conditions, and discourage it by pointing to the opposite. These same arguments also form the materials for accusation or defence -- the deterrents being pointed out by the defence, and the inducements by the prosecution. As for the defence,....This topic forms the whole Art of Rhetoric both of Pamphilus and of Callippus.

21. Another line of argument refers to things which are supposed to happen and yet seem incredible. We may argue that people could not have believed them, if they had not been true or nearly true: even that they are the more likely to be true because they are incredible. For the things which men believe are either facts or probabilities: if, therefore, a thing that is believed is improbable and even incredible, it must be true, since it is certainly not believed because it is at all probable or credible. An example is what Androcles of the deme Pitthus said in his well-known arraignment of the law. The audience tried to shout him down when he observed that the laws required a law to set them right. "Why," he went on, "fish need salt, improbable and incredible as this might seem for creatures reared in salt water; and olive-cakes need oil, incredible as it is that what produces oil should need it."

22. Another line of argument is to refute our opponent's case by noting any contrasts or contradictions of dates, acts, or words that it anywhere displays; and this in any of the three following connexions. (1) Referring to our opponent's conduct, e.g. "He says he is devoted to you, yet he conspired with the Thirty." (2) Referring to our own conduct, e.g. "He says I am litigious, and yet he cannot prove that I have been engaged in a single lawsuit." (3) Referring to both of us together, e.g. "He has never even lent any one a penny, but I have ransomed quite a

number of you."

23. Another line that is useful for men and causes that have been really or seemingly slandered, is to show why the facts are not as supposed; pointing out that there is a reason for the false impression given. Thus a woman, who had palmed off her son on another woman, was thought to be the lad's mistress because she embraced him; but when her action was explained the charge was shown to be groundless. Another example is from the Ajax of Theodectes, where Odysseus tells Ajax the reason why, though he is really braver than Ajax, he is not thought so.

24. Another line of argument is to show that if the cause is present, the effect is present, and if absent, absent. For by proving the cause you at once prove the effect, and conversely nothing can exist without its cause. Thus Thrasybulus accused Leodamas of having had his name recorded as a criminal on the slab in the Acropolis, and of erasing the record in the time of the Thirty Tyrants: to which Leodamas replied, "Impossible: for the Thirty would have trusted me all the more if my quarrel with the commons had been inscribed on the slab."

25. Another line is to consider whether the accused person can take or could have taken a better course than that which he is recommending or taking, or has taken. If he has not taken this better course, it is clear that he is not guilty, since no one deliberately and consciously chooses what is bad. This argument is, however, fallacious, for it often becomes clear after the event how the action could have been done better, though before the event this was far from clear.

26. Another line is, when a contemplated action is inconsistent with any past action, to examine them both together. Thus, when the people of Elea asked Xenophanes if they should or should not sacrificeto Leucothea and mourn for her, he advised them not to mourn for her if they thought her a goddess, and not to sacrifice to her if they thought her a mortal woman.

27. Another line is to make previous mistakes the grounds of accusation or defence. Thus, in the Medea of Carcinus the accusers allege that Medea has slain her children; "at all events," they say,"they are not to be seen" -- Medea having made the mistake of sending her children away. In defence she argues that it is not her children, but Jason, whom she would have slain; for it would have been a mistake on her part not to do this if she had done the other. This special line of argument for enthymeme forms the whole of the Art of Rhetoric in use before Theodorus. Another line is to draw meanings from names. Sophocles, forinstance, says,

O steel in heart as thou art steel in name.

This line of argument is common in praises of the gods. Thus, too, Conon called Thrasybulus rash in counsel. And Herodicus said of Thrasymachus, "You are always bold in battle"; of Polus, "you are always a colt"; and of the legislator Draco that his laws were those not of a human being but of a dragon, so savage were they. And, in Euripides, Hecuba says of Aphrodite,

Her name and Folly's (aphrosuns) lightly begin alike,

and Chaeremon writes

Pentheus -- aname foreshadowing grief (penthos) to come.

The Refutative Enthymeme has a greater reputation than the Demonstrative, because within a small space it works out two opposing arguments, and arguments put side by side are clearer to the audience. But of all syllogisms, whether refutative or demonstrative, those are most applauded of which we foresee the conclusions from the beginning, so long as they are not obvious at first sight -- for part of the pleasure we feel is at our own intelligent anticipation; or those which we follow well enough to see the point ofthem as soon as the last word has been uttered.

Part 24

Besides genuine syllogisms, there may be syllogisms that look genuine but are not; and since an enthymeme is merely a syllogism of a particular kind, it follows that, besides genuine enthymemes, there may be those that look genuine but are not.

1. Among the lines of argument that form the Spurious Enthymeme the first is that which arises from the particular words employed.

(a) One variety of this is when -- as in dialectic, without having gone through any reasoning process, we make a final statement as if it were the conclusion of such a process, "Therefore so-and-so is not true," "Therefore also so-and-so must be true" -- so too in rhetoric a compact and antithetical utterance passes for an enthymeme, such language being the proper province of enthymeme, so that it is seemingly the form of wording here that causes the illusion mentioned. In order to produce the effect of genuine reasoning by our form of wording it is useful to summarize the results of a number of previous reasonings: as "some he saved -- others he avenged -- the Greeks he freed." Each of these statements has been previously proved from other facts; but the mere collocation of them gives the impression of establishing some fresh conclusion.

(b) Another variety is based on the use of similar words for different things; e.g. the argument that the mouse must be a noble creature, since it gives its name to the most august of all religious rites -- for such the Mysteries are. Or one may introduce, into a eulogy of the dog, the dog-star; or Pan, because Pindar said:

O thou blessed one!
Thou whom they of Olympus call
The hound of manifold shape
That follows the Mother of Heaven:

or we may argue that, because there is much disgrace in there not being a dog about, there is honour in being a dog. Or that Hermes is readier than any other god to go shares, since we never say "shares all round" except of him. Or that speech is a very excellent thing, since good men are not said to be worth money but to be worthy of esteem -- the phrase "worthy of esteem" also having the meaning of "worth speech."

2. Another line is to assert of the whole what is true of the parts, or of the parts what is true of the whole. A whole and its parts are supposed to be identical, though often they are not. You have therefore to adopt whichever of these two lines better suits your purpose. That is how Euthydemus argues: e.g. that any one knows that there is a trireme in the Peiraeus, since he knows the separate details that make up this statement. There is also the argument that one who knows the letters knows the whole word, since the word is the same thing as the letters which compose it; or that, if a double portion of a certain thing is harmful to health, then a single portion must not be called wholesome, since it is absurd that two good things should make one bad thing. Put thus, the enthymeme is refutative; put as follows; demonstrative: "For one good thing cannot be made up of two bad things." The whole line of argument is fallacious. Again, there is Polycrates' saying that Thrasybulus put down thirty tyrants, where the speaker adds them up one by one. Or the argument in the Orestes of Theodectes, where the argument is from part to whole:

'Tis right that she who slays her lord should die.

"It is right, too, that the son should avenge his father. Very good: these two things are what Orestes has done." Still, perhaps the two things, once they are put together, do not form a right act. The fallacy might also be said to be due to omission, since the speaker fails to say by whose hand a husband-slayer should die.

3. Another line is the use of indignant language, whether to support your own case or to overthrow your opponent's. We do this when we paint a highly-coloured picture of the situation without having proved the facts of it: if the defendant does so, he produces an impression of his innocence; and if the prosecutor goes into a passion, he produces an impression of the defendant's guilt. Here there is no genuine enthymeme: the hearer infers guilt or innocence, but no proof is given, and the inference is fallacious accordingly.

4. Another line is to use a "Sign," or single instance, as certain evidence; which, again, yields no valid proof. Thus, it might be said that lovers are useful to their countries, since the love of Harmodius and Aristogeiton caused the downfall of the tyrant Hipparchus. Or, again, that Dionysius is a thief, since he is a vicious man -- there is, of course, no valid proof here; not every vicious man is a thief, though every thief is a vicious man.

5. Another line represents the accidental as essential. An instance is what Polycrates says of the mice, that they "came to the rescue" because they gnawed through the bowstrings. Or it might be maintained that an invitation to dinner is a great honour, for it was because he was not invited that Achilles was "angered" with the Greeks at Tenedos? As a fact, what angered him was the insult involved; it was a mere accident that this was the particular form that the insult took.

6. Another is the argument from consequence. In the Alexander, for instance, it is argued that Paris must have had a lofty disposition, since he despised society and lived by himself on Mount Ida: because lofty people do this kind of thing, therefore Paris too, we are to suppose, had a lofty

soul. Or, if a man dresses fashionably and roams around at night, he is a rake, since that is the way rakes behave. Another similar argument points out that beggars sing and dance in temples, and that exiles can live wherever they please, and that such privileges are at the disposal of those we account happy and therefore every one might be regarded as happy if only he has those privileges. What matters, however, is the circumstances under which the privileges are enjoyed. Hence this line too falls under the head of fallacies by omission.

7. Another line consists in representing as causes things which are not causes, on the ground that they happened along with or before the event in question. They assume that, because B happens after A, it happens because of A. Politicians are especially fond of taking this line. Thus Demades said that the policy of Demosthenes was the cause of all the mischief, "for after it the war occurred."

8. Another line consists in leaving out any mention of time and circumstances. E.g. the argument that Paris was justified in taking Helen, since her father left her free to choose: here the freedom was presumably not perpetual; it could only refer to her first choice, beyond which her father's authority could not go. Or again, one might say that to strike a free man is an act of wanton outrage; but it is not so in every case -- only when it is unprovoked.

9. Again, a spurious syllogism may, as in "eristical" discussions, be based on the confusion of the absolute with that which is not absolute but particular. As, in dialectic, for instance, it may be argued that what-is-not is, on the ground that what-is-not is what-is-not: or that the unknown can be known, on the ground that it can be known to be unknown: so also in rhetoric a spurious enthymeme may be based on the confusion of some particular probability with absolute probability. Now no particular probability is universally probable: as Agathon says,

> One might perchance say that was probable --
> That things improbable oft will hap to men.

For what is improbable does happen, and therefore it is probable that improbable things will happen. Granted this, one might argue that "what is improbable is probable." But this is not true absolutely. As, in eristic, the imposture comes from not adding any clause specifying relationship or reference or manner; so here it arises because the probability in question is not general but specific. It is of this line of argument that Corax's Art of Rhetoric is composed. If the accused is not open to the charge -- for instance if a weakling be tried for violent assault -- the defence is that he was not likely to do such a thing. But if he is open to the charge -- i.e. if he is a strong man -- the defence is still that he was not likely to do such a thing, since he could be sure that people would think he was likely to do it. And so with any other charge: the accused must be either open or not open to it: there is in either case an appearance of probable innocence, but whereas in the latter case the probability is genuine, in the former it can only be asserted in the special sense mentioned. This sort of argument illustrates what is meant by making the worse argument seem the better. Hence people were right in objecting to the training Protagoras undertook to give them. It was a fraud; the probability it handled was not genuine but spurious, and has a place in no art except Rhetoric and Eristic.

Part 25

Enthymemes, genuine and apparent, have now been described; the next subject is their Refutation.

An argument may be refuted either by a counter-syllogism or by bringing an objection. It is clear that counter-syllogisms can be built up from the same lines of arguments as the original syllogisms: for the materials of syllogisms are the ordinary opinions of men, and such opinions often contradict each other. Objections, as appears in the Topics, may be raised in four ways -- either by directly attacking your opponent's own statement, or by putting forward another statement like it, or by putting forward a statement contrary to it, or by quoting previous decisions.

1. By "attacking your opponent's own statement" I mean, for instance, this: if his enthymeme should assert that love is always good, the objection can be brought in two ways, either by making the general statement that "all want is an evil," or by making the particular one that there would be no talk of "Caunian love" if there were not evil loves as well as good ones.

2. An objection "from a contrary statement" is raised when, for instance, the opponent's enthymeme having concluded that a good man does good to all his friends, you object, "That proves nothing, for a bad man does not do evil to all his friends."

3. An example of an objection "from a like statement" is, the enthymeme having shown that ill-used men always hate their ill-users, to reply, "That proves nothing, for well-used men do not always love those who used them well."

4. The "decisions" mentioned are those proceeding from well-known men; for instance, if the enthymeme employed has concluded that "that allowance ought to be made for drunken offenders, since they did not know what they were doing," the objection will be, "Pittacus, then, deserves no approval, or he would not have prescribed specially severe penalties for offences due to drunkenness."

Enthymemes are based upon one or other of four kinds of alleged fact: (1) Probabilities, (2) Examples, (3) Infallible Signs, (4) Ordinary Signs. (1) Enthymemes based upon Probabilities are those which argue from what is, or is supposed to be, usually true. (2) Enthymemes based upon Example are those which proceed by induction from one or more similar cases, arrive at a general proposition, and then argue deductively to a particular inference. (3) Enthymemes based upon Infallible Signs are those which argue from the inevitable and invariable. (4) Enthymemes based upon ordinary Signs are those which argue from some universal or particular proposition, true or false.

Now (1) as a Probability is that which happens usually but not always, Enthymemes founded upon Probabilities can, it is clear, always be refuted by raising some objection. The refutation is not always genuine: it may be spurious: for it consists in showing not that your opponent's premiss is not probable, but Only in showing that it is not inevitably true. Hence it is always in defence rather than in accusation that it is possible to gain an advantage by using this fallacy. For the accuser uses probabilities to prove his case: and to refute a conclusion as improbable is not the same thing as to refute it as not inevitable. Any argument based upon what usually happens is always open to objection: otherwise it would not be a probability but an invariable and necessary truth. But the judges think, if the refutation takes this form, either that the accuser's case is not probable or that they must not decide it; which, as we said, is a false piece of reasoning. For they ought to decide by considering not merely what must be true but also what is likely to be true: this is, indeed, the meaning of "giving a verdict in accordance with one's honest opinion." Therefore it is not enough for the defendant to refute the accusation by proving that the charge is not bound to be true: he must do so by showing that it is not likely to be true. For this purpose his objection must state what is more usually true than the statement attacked. It may do so in either of two ways: either in respect of frequency or in respect of exactness. It will be most convincing if it does so in both respects; for if the thing in question both happens oftener as we represent it and happens more as we represent it, the probability is particularly great.

(2) Fallible Signs, and Enthymemes based upon them, can be refuted even if the facts are correct, as was said at the outset. For we have shown in the Analytics that no Fallible Sign can form part of a valid logical proof.

(3) Enthymemes depending on examples may be refuted in the same way as probabilities. If we have a negative instance, the argument is refuted, in so far as it is proved not inevitable, even though the positive examples are more similar and more frequent. And if the positive examples are more numerous and more frequent, we must contend that the present case is dissimilar, or that its conditions are dissimilar, or that it is different in some way or other.

(4) It will be impossible to refute Infallible Signs, and Enthymemes resting on them, by showing in any way that they do not form a valid logical proof: this, too, we see from the Analytics. All we can do is to show that the fact alleged does not exist. If there is no doubt that it does, and that it is an Infallible Sign, refutation now becomes impossible: for this is equivalent to a demonstration which is clear in every respect.

Part 26

Amplification and Depreciation are not an element of enthymeme. By "an element of enthymeme" I mean the same thing as a line of enthymematic argument -- a general class embracing a large number of particular kinds of enthymeme. Amplification and Depreciation are one kind of enthymeme, viz. the kind used to show that a thing is great or small; just as there are other kinds used to show that a thing is good or bad, just or unjust, and anything else of the sort. All these things are the subject-matter of syllogisms and enthymemes; none of these is the line of argument of an enthymeme; no more, therefore, are Amplification and Depreciation. Nor are Refutative Enthymemes a different species from Constructive. For it is clear that refutation consists either in offering positive proof or in raising an objection. In the first case we prove the opposite of our adversary's statements. Thus, if he shows that a thing has happened, we show that it has not; if he shows that it has not happened, we show that it has. This, then, could not be the distinction if there were one, since the same means are employed by both parties, enthymemes being adduced to show that the fact is or is not so-and-so. An objection, on the other hand, is not an enthymeme at all, as was said in the Topics, consists in stating some accepted opinion from which it will be clear that our opponent has not reasoned correctly or has made a false assumption.

Three points must be studied in making a speech; and we have now completed the account of (1) Examples, Maxims, Enthymemes, and in general the thought-element -- the way to invent and refute arguments. [1403b] We have next to discuss (2) Style, and (3) Arrangement.

BOOK III

Part 1

In making a speech one must study three points: first, the means of producing persuasion; second, the style, or language, to be used; third, the proper arrangement of the various parts of the speech. We have already specified the sources of persuasion. We have shown that these are three in number; what they are; and why there are only these three: for we have shown that persuasion must in every case be effected either (1) by working on the emotions of the judges themselves, (2) by giving them the right impression of the speakers' character, or (3) by proving the truth of the statements made.

Enthymemes also have been described, and the sources from which they should be derived; there being both special and general lines of argument for enthymemes.

Our next subject will be the style of expression. For it is not enough to know what we ought to say; we must also say it as we ought; much help is thus afforded towards producing the right impression of a speech. The first question to receive attention was naturally the one that comes first naturally-how persuasion can be produced from the facts themselves. The second is how to set these facts out in language. A third would be the proper method of delivery; this is a thing that affects the success of a speech greatly; but hitherto the subject has been neglected. Indeed, it was long before it found a way into the arts of tragic drama and epic recitation: at first poets acted their tragedies themselves. It is plain that delivery has just as much to do with oratory as with poetry. (In connexion with poetry, it has been studied by Glaucon of Teos among others.) It is, essentially, a matter of the right management of the voice to express the various emotions-of speaking loudly, softly, or between the two; of high, low, or intermediate pitch; of the various rhythms that suit various subjects. These are the three things-volume of sound, modulation of pitch, and rhythm-that a speaker bears in mind. It is those who do bear them in mind who usually win prizes in the dramatic contests; and just as in drama the actors now count for more than the poets, so it is in the contests of public life, owing to the defects of our political institutions. No systematic treatise upon the rules of delivery has yet been composed; indeed, even the study of language made no progress till late in the day. Besides, delivery is-very properly-not regarded as an elevated subject of inquiry. Still, the whole business of rhetoric being concerned with appearances, we must pay attention to the subject of delivery, unworthy though it is, because we cannot do without it. The right thing in speaking really is that we should be satisfied not to annoy our hearers, without trying to delight them: we ought in fairness to fight our case with no help beyond the bare facts: nothing, therefore, should matter except the proof of those facts. Still, as has been already said, other things affect the result considerably, owing to the defects of our hearers. The arts of language cannot help having a small but real importance, whatever it is we have to expound to others: the way in which a thing is said does affect its intelligibility. Not, however, so much importance as people think. All such arts are fanciful and meant to charm the hearer. Nobody uses fine language when teaching geometry.

When the principles of delivery have been worked out, they will produce the same effect as on the stage. But only very slight attempts to deal with them have been made and by a few people, as by Thrasymachus in his 'Appeals to Pity'. Dramatic ability is a natural gift, and can hardly be systematically taught. The principles of good diction can be so taught, and therefore we have men of ability in this direction too, who win prizes in their turn, as well as those speakers who excel in delivery-speeches of the written or literary kind owe more of their effect to their direction than to their thought.

It was naturally the poets who first set the movement going; for words represent things, and they had also the human voice at their disposal, which of all our organs can best represent other things. Thus the arts of recitation and acting were formed, and others as well. Now it was because poets seemed to win fame through their fine language when their thoughts were simple enough, that the language of oratorical prose at first took a poetical colour, e.g. that of Gorgias. Even now most uneducated people think that poetical language makes the finest discourses. That is not true: the language of prose is distinct from that of poetry. This is shown by the state of things to-day, when even the language of tragedy has altered its character. Just as iambics were adopted, instead of tetrameters, because they are the most prose-like of all metres, so tragedy has given up all those words, not used in ordinary talk, which decorated the early drama and are still used by the writers of hexameter poems. It is therefore ridiculous to imitate a poetical manner which the poets themselves have dropped; and it is now plain that we have not to treat in detail the whole question of style, but may confine ourselves to that part of it which concerns our present subject, rhetoric. The other--the poetical--part of it has been discussed in the treatise on the Art of Poetry.

Part 2

We may, then, start from the observations there made, including the definition of style. Style to be good must be clear, as is proved by the fact that speech which fails to convey a plain meaning will fail to do just what speech has to do. It must also be appropriate, avoiding both meanness and undue elevation; poetical language is certainly free from meanness, but it is not appropriate to prose. Clearness is secured by using the words (nouns and verbs alike) that are current and ordinary. Freedom from meanness, and positive adornment too, are secured by using the other words mentioned in the Art of Poetry. Such variation from what is usual makes the language appear more stately. People do not feel towards strangers as they do towards their own countrymen, and the same thing is true of their feeling for language. It is therefore well to give to everyday speech an unfamiliar air: people like what strikes them, and are struck by what is out of the way. In verse such effects are common, and there they are fitting: the persons and things there spoken of are comparatively remote from ordinary life. In prose passages they are far less often fitting because the subject-matter is less exalted. Even in poetry, it is not quite appropriate that fine language should be used by a slave or a very young man, or about very trivial subjects: even in poetry the style, to be appropriate, must sometimes be toned down, though at other times heightened. We can now see that a writer must disguise his art and give the impression of speaking naturally and not artificially. Naturalness is persuasive, artificiality is the contrary; for our hearers are prejudiced and think we have some design against them, as if we were mixing their wines for them. It is like the difference between the quality of Theodorus' voice and the voices of all other actors: his really seems to be that of the character who is speaking, theirs do not. We can hide our purpose successfully by taking the single words of our composition from the speech of ordinary life. This is done in poetry by Euripides, who was the first to show the way to his successors.

Language is composed of nouns and verbs. Nouns are of the various kinds considered in the treatise on Poetry. Strange words, compound words, and invented words must be used sparingly and on few occasions: on what occasions we shall state later. The reason for this restriction has been already indicated: they depart from what is suitable, in the direction of excess. In the language of prose, besides the regular and proper terms for things, metaphorical terms only can be used with advantage. This we gather from the fact that these two classes of terms, the proper or regular and the metaphorical-these and no others-are used by everybody in conversation. We can now see that a good writer can produce a style that is distinguished without being obtrusive, and is at the same time clear, thus satisfying our definition of good oratorical prose. Words of ambiguous meaning are chiefly useful to enable the sophist to mislead his hearers. Synonyms are useful to the poet, by which I mean words whose ordinary meaning is the same, e.g. 'porheueseai' (advancing) and 'badizein' (proceeding); these two are ordinary words and have the same meaning.

In the Art of Poetry, as we have already said, will be found definitions of these kinds of words; a classification of Metaphors; and mention of the fact that metaphor is of great value both in poetry and in prose. Prose-writers must, however, pay specially careful attention to metaphor, because their other resources are scantier than those of poets. Metaphor, moreover, gives style clearness, charm, and distinction as nothing else can: and it is not a thing whose use can be taught by one man to another. Metaphors, like epithets, must be fitting, which means that they must fairly correspond to the thing signified: failing this, their inappropriateness will be conspicuous: the want of harmony between two things is emphasized by their being placed side by side. It is like having to ask ourselves what dress will suit an old man; certainly not the crimson cloak that suits a young man. And if you wish to pay a compliment, you must take your metaphor from something better in the same line; if to disparage, from something worse. To illustrate my meaning: since opposites are in the same class, you do what I have suggested if you say that a man who begs 'prays', and a man who prays 'begs'; for praying and begging are both varieties of asking. So Iphicrates called Callias a 'mendicant priest' instead of a 'torch-bearer', and Callias replied that Iphicrates must be uninitiated or he would have called him not a 'mendicant priest' but a 'torch-bearer'. Both are religious titles, but one is honourable and the other is not. Again, somebody calls actors 'hangers-on of Dionysus', but they call themselves 'artists': each of these terms is a metaphor, the one intended to throw dirt at the actor, the other to dignify him. And pirates now call themselves 'purveyors'. We can thus call a crime a mistake, or a mistake a crime. We can say that a thief 'took' a thing, or that he 'plundered' his victim. An expression like that of Euripides' Telephus,

"King of the oar, on Mysia's coast he landed, "

is inappropriate; the word 'king' goes beyond the dignity of the subject, and so the art is not concealed. A metaphor may be amiss because the very syllables of the words conveying it fail to indicate sweetness of vocal utterance. Thus Dionysius the Brazen in his elegies calls poetry 'Calliope's screech'. Poetry and screeching are both, to be sure, vocal utterances. But the metaphor is bad, because the sounds of 'screeching', unlike those of poetry, are discordant and unmeaning. Further, in using metaphors to give names to nameless things, we must draw them not from remote but from kindred and similar things, so that the kinship is clearly perceived as soon as the words are said. Thus in the celebrated riddle

"I marked how a man glued bronze with fire to another man's body, "

the process is nameless; but both it and gluing are a kind of application, and that is why the application of the cupping-glass is here called a 'gluing'. Good riddles do, in general, provide us with satisfactory metaphors: for metaphors imply riddles, and therefore a good riddle can furnish a good metaphor. Further, the materials of metaphors must be beautiful; and the beauty, like the ugliness, of all words may, as Licymnius says, lie in their sound or in their meaning. Further, there is a third consideration-one that upsets the fallacious argument of the sophist Bryson, that there is no such thing as foul language, because in whatever words you put a given thing your meaning is the same. This is untrue. One term may describe a thing more truly than another, may be more like it, and set it more intimately before our eyes. Besides, two different words will represent a thing in two different lights; so on this ground also one term must be held fairer or fouler than another. For both of two terms will indicate what is fair, or what is foul, but not simply their fairness or their foulness, or if so, at any rate not in an equal degree. The materials of metaphor must be beautiful to the ear, to the understanding, to the eye or some other physical sense. It is better, for instance, to say 'rosy-fingered morn', than 'crimson-fingered' or, worse still, 'red-fingered morn'. The epithets that we apply, too, may have a bad and ugly aspect, as when

Orestes is called a 'mother-slayer'; or a better one, as when he is called his 'father's avenger'. Simonides, when the victor in the mule-race offered him a small fee, refused to write him an ode, because, he said, it was so unpleasant to write odes to half-asses: but on receiving an adequate fee, he wrote

"Hail to you, daughters of storm-footed steeds? "

though of course they were daughters of asses too. The same effect is attained by the use of diminutives, which make a bad thing less bad and a good thing less good. Take, for instance, the banter of Aristophanes in the Babylonians where he uses 'goldlet' for 'gold', 'cloaklet' for 'cloak', 'scoffiet' for 'scoff, and 'plaguelet'. But alike in using epithets and in using diminutives we must be wary and must observe the mean.

Part 3

Bad taste in language may take any of four forms:
(1) The misuse of compound words. Lycophron, for instance, talks of the 'many visaged heaven' above the 'giant-crested earth', and again the 'strait-pathed shore'; and Gorgias of the 'pauper-poet flatterer' and 'oath-breaking and over-oath-keeping'. Alcidamas uses such expressions as 'the soul filling with rage and face becoming flame-flushed', and 'he thought their enthusiasm would be issue-fraught' and 'issue-fraught he made the persuasion of his words', and 'sombre-hued is the floor of the sea'.The way all these words are compounded makes them, we feel, fit for verse only. This, then, is one form in which bad taste is shown.

(2) Another is the employment of strange words. For instance, Lycophron talks of 'the prodigious Xerxes' and 'spoliative Sciron'; Alcidamas of 'a toy for poetry' and 'the witlessness of nature', and says 'whetted with the unmitigated temper of his spirit'.

(3) A third form is the use of long, unseasonable, or frequent epithets. It is appropriate enough for a poet to talk of 'white milk', in prose such epithets are sometimes lacking in appropriateness or, when spread too thickly, plainly reveal the author turning his prose into poetry. Of course we must use some epithets, since they lift our style above the usual level and give it an air of distinction. But we must aim at the due mean, or the result will be worse than if we took no trouble at all; we shall get something actually bad instead of something merely not good. That is why the epithets of Alcidamas seem so tasteless; he does not use them as the seasoning of the meat, but as the meat itself, so numerous and swollen and aggressive are they. For instance, he does not say 'sweat', but 'the moist sweat'; not 'to the Isthmian games', but 'to the world-concourse of the Isthmian games'; not 'laws', but 'the laws that are monarchs of states'; not 'at a run', but 'his heart impelling him to speed of foot'; not 'a school of the Muses', but 'Nature's school of the Muses had he inherited'; and so 'frowning care of heart', and 'achiever' not of 'popularity' but of 'universal popularity', and 'dispenser of pleasure to his audience', and 'he concealed it' not 'with boughs' but 'with boughs of the forest trees', and 'he clothed' not 'his body' but 'his body's nakedness', and 'his soul's desire was counter imitative' (this's at one and the same

time a compound and an epithet, so that it seems a poet's effort), and 'so extravagant the excess of his wickedness'. We thus see how the inappropriateness of such poetical language imports absurdity and tastelessness into speeches, as well as the obscurity that comes from all this verbosity-for when the sense is plain, you only obscure and spoil its clearness by piling up words.

The ordinary use of compound words is where there is no term for a thing and some compound can be easily formed, like 'pastime' (chronotribein); but if this is much done, the prose character disappears entirely. We now see why the language of compounds is just the thing for writers of dithyrambs, who love sonorous noises; strange words for writers of epic poetry, which is a proud and stately affair; and metaphor for iambic verse, the metre which (as has been already' said) is widely used to-day.

(4) There remains the fourth region in which bad taste may be shown, metaphor. Metaphors like other things may be inappropriate. Some are so because they are ridiculous; they are indeed used by comic as well as tragic poets. Others are too grand and theatrical; and these, if they are far-fetched, may also be obscure. For instance, Gorgias talks of 'events that are green and full of sap', and says 'foul was the deed you sowed and evil the harvest you reaped'. That is too much like poetry. Alcidamas, again, called philosophy 'a fortress that threatens the power of law', and the Odyssey 'a goodly looking-glass of human life',' talked about 'offering no such toy to poetry': all these expressions fail, for the reasons given, to carry the hearer with them. The address of Gorgias to the swallow, when she had let her droppings fall on him as she flew overhead, is in the best tragic manner. He said, 'Nay, shame, O Philomela'. Considering her as a bird, you could not call her act shameful; considering her as a girl, you could; and so it was a good gibe to address her as what she was once and not as what she is.

Part 4

The Simile also is a metaphor; the difference is but slight. When the poet says of Achilles that he

"Leapt on the foe as a lion, "

this is a simile; when he says of him 'the lion leapt', it is a metaphor-here, since both are courageous, he has transferred to Achilles the name of 'lion'. Similes are useful in prose as well as in verse; but not often, since they are of the nature of poetry. They are to be employed just as metaphors are employed, since they are really the same thing except for the difference mentioned.

The following are examples of similes. Androtion said of Idrieus that he was like a terrier let off the chain, that flies at you and bites you-Idrieus too was savage now that he was let out of his chains. Theodamas compared Archidamus to an Euxenus who could not do geometry-a proportional simile, implying that Euxenus is an Archidamus who can do geometry. In Plato's Republic those who strip the dead are compared to curs which bite the stones thrown at them but do not touch the thrower, and there is the simile about the Athenian people, who are compared to a ship's captain who is strong but a little deaf; and the one about poets' verses, which are likened to persons who lack beauty but possess youthful freshness-when the freshness has faded the charm perishes, and so with verses when broken up into prose. Pericles compared the Samians to children who take their pap but go on crying; and the Boeotians to holm-oaks, because they were ruining one another by civil wars just as one oak causes another oak's fall. Demosthenes said that the Athenian people were like sea-sick men on board ship. Again, Demosthenes compared the political orators to nurses who swallow the bit of food themselves and then smear the children's lips with the spittle. Antisthenes compared the lean Cephisodotus to frankincense, because it was his consumption that gave one pleasure. All these ideas may be expressed either as similes or as metaphors; those which succeed as metaphors will obviously do well also as similes, and similes, with the explanation omitted, will appear as metaphors. But the proportional metaphor must always apply reciprocally to either of its co-ordinate terms. For instance, if a drinking-bowl is the shield of Dionysus, a shield may fittingly be called the drinking-bowl of Ares.

Part 5

Such, then, are the ingredients of which speech is composed. The foundation of good style is correctness of language, which falls under five heads. (1) First, the proper use of connecting words, and the arrangement of them in the natural sequence which some of them require. For instance, the connective 'men' (e.g. ego men) requires the correlative de (e.g. o de). The answering word must be brought in before the first has been forgotten, and not be widely separated from it; nor, except in the few cases where this is appropriate, is another connective to be introduced before the one required. Consider the sentence, 'But as soon as he told me (for Cleon had come begging and praying), took them along and set out.' In this sentence many connecting words are inserted in front of the one required to complete the sense; and if there is a long interval before 'set out', the result is obscurity. One merit, then, of good style lies in the right use of connecting words. (2) The second lies in calling things by their own special names and not by vague general ones. (3) The third is to avoid ambiguities; unless, indeed, you definitely desire to be ambiguous, as those do who have nothing to say but are pretending to mean something. Such people are apt to put that sort of thing into verse. Empedocles, for instance, by his long circumlocutions imposes on his hearers; these are affected in the same way as most people are when they listen to diviners, whose ambiguous utterances are received with nods of acquiescence-

"Croesus by crossing the Halys will ruin a mighty realm. "

Diviners use these vague generalities about the matter in hand because their predictions are thus, as a rule, less likely to be falsified. We are more likely to be right, in the game of 'odd and even', if we simply guess 'even' or 'odd' than if we guess at the actual number; and the oracle-monger is more likely to be right if he simply says that a thing will happen than if he says when it will happen, and therefore he refuses to add a definite date. All these ambiguities have the same sort of effect, and are to be avoided unless we have some such object as that mentioned. (4) A fourth rule is to observe Protagoras' classification of nouns into male, female, and inanimate; for these distinctions also must be correctly given. 'Upon her arrival she said her say and departed (e d elthousa kai dialechtheisa ocheto).' (5) A fifth rule is to express plurality, fewness, and unity by the correct wording, e.g. 'Having come, they struck me (oi d elthontes etupton me).'

It is a general rule that a written composition should be easy to read and therefore easy to deliver. This cannot be so where there are many connecting words or clauses, or where punctuation is hard, as in the writings of Heracleitus. To punctuate Heracleitus is no easy task, because we often cannot tell whether a particular word belongs to what precedes or what follows it. Thus, at the outset of his treatise he says, 'Though this truth is always men understand it not', where it is not clear with which of the two clauses the word 'always' should be joined by the punctuation. Further, the following fact leads to solecism, viz. that the sentence does not work out properly if you annex to two terms a third which does not suit them both. Thus either 'sound' or 'colour' will fail to work out properly with some verbs: 'perceive' will apply to both, 'see' will not. Obscurity is also caused if, when you intend to insert a number of details, you do not first make your meaning clear; for instance, if you say, 'I meant, after telling him this, that and the other thing, to set out', rather than something of this kind 'I meant to set out after telling him; then this, that, and the other thing occurred.'

Part 6

The following suggestions will help to give your language impressiveness. (1) Describe a thing instead of naming it: do not say 'circle', but 'that surface which extends equally from the middle every way'. To achieve conciseness, do the opposite-put the name instead of the description. When mentioning anything ugly or unseemly, use its name if it is the description that is ugly, and describe it if it is the name that is ugly. (2) Represent things with the help of metaphors and epithets, being careful to avoid poetical effects. (3) Use plural for singular, as in poetry, where one finds

"Unto havens Achaean, "

though only one haven is meant, and

"Here are my letter's many-leaved folds. "

(4) Do not bracket two words under one article, but put one article with each; e.g. 'that wife of ours.' The reverse to secure conciseness; e.g. 'our wife.' Use plenty of connecting words; conversely, to secure conciseness, dispense with connectives, while still preserving connexion; e.g. 'having gone and spoken', and 'having gone, I spoke', respectively. (6) And the practice of Antimachus, too, is useful-to describe a thing by mentioning attributes it does not possess; as he does in talking of Teumessus

"There is a little wind-swept knoll... "

A subject can be developed indefinitely along these lines. You may apply this method of treatment by negation either to good or to bad qualities, according to which your subject requires. It is from this source that the poets draw expressions such as the 'stringless' or 'lyreless' melody, thus forming epithets out of negations. This device is popular in proportional metaphors, as when the trumpet's note is called 'a lyreless melody'.

Part 7

Your language will be appropriate if it expresses emotion and character, and if it corresponds to its subject. 'Correspondence to subject' means that we must neither speak casually about weighty matters, nor solemnly about trivial ones; nor must we add ornamental epithets to commonplace nouns, or the effect will be comic, as in the works of Cleophon, who can use phrases as absurd as 'O queenly fig-tree'. To express emotion, you will employ the language of anger in speaking of outrage; the language of disgust and discreet reluctance to utter a word when speaking of impiety or foulness; the language of exultation for a tale of glory, and that of humiliation for a tale of and so in all other cases.

This aptness of language is one thing that makes people believe in the truth of your story: their minds draw the false conclusion that you are to be trusted from the fact that others behave as you do when things are as you describe them; and therefore they take your story to be true, whether it is so or not. Besides, an emotional speaker always makes his audience feel with him, even when there is nothing in his arguments; which is why many speakers try to overwhelm their audience by mere noise.

Furthermore, this way of proving your story by displaying these signs of its genuineness expresses your personal character. Each class of men, each type of disposition, will have its own appropriate way of letting the truth appear. Under 'class' I include differences of age, as boy, man, or old man; of sex, as man or woman; of nationality, as Spartan or Thessalian. By 'dispositions' I here mean those dispositions only which determine the character of a man's for it is not every disposition that does this. If, then, a speaker uses the very words which are in keeping with a particular disposition, he will reproduce the corresponding character; for a rustic and an educated man will not say the same things nor speak in the same way. Again, some impression is made upon an audience by a device which speech-writers employ to nauseous excess, when they say 'Who does not know this?' or 'It is known to everybody.' The hearer is ashamed of his ignorance, and agrees with the speaker, so as to have a share of the knowledge that everybody else possesses.

All the variations of oratorical style are capable of being used in season or out of season. The best way to counteract any exaggeration is the well-worn device by which the speaker puts in some criticism of himself; for then people feel it must be all right for him to talk thus, since he certainly knows what he is doing. Further, it is better not to have everything always just corresponding to everything else-your hearers will see through you less easily thus. I mean for instance, if your words are harsh, you should not extend this harshness to your voice and your countenance and have everything else in keeping. If you do, the artificial character of each detail becomes apparent; whereas if you adopt one device and not another, you are using art all the same and yet nobody notices it. (To be sure, if mild sentiments are expressed in harsh tones and harsh sentiments in mild tones, you become comparatively unconvincing.) Compound words, fairly plentiful epithets, and strange words best suit an emotional speech. We forgive an angry man for talking about a wrong as 'heaven-high' or 'colossal'; and we excuse such language when the speaker has his hearers already in his hands and has stirred them deeply either by praise or blame or anger or affection, as Isocrates, for instance, does at the end of his Panegyric, with his 'name and fame' and 'in that they brooked'. Men do speak in this strain when they are deeply stirred, and so, once the audience is in a like state of feeling, approval of course follows. This is why such language is fitting in poetry, which is an inspired thing. This language, then, should be used either under stress of emotion, or ironically, after the manner of Gorgias and of the passages in the Phaedrus.

Part 8

The form of a prose composition should be neither metrical nor destitute of rhythm. The metrical form destroys the hearer's trust by its artificial appearance, and at the same time it diverts his attention, making him watch for metrical recurrences, just as children catch up the herald's question, 'Whom does the freedman choose as his advocate?', with the answer 'Cleon!' On the other hand, unrhythmical language is too unlimited; we do not want the limitations of metre, but some limitation we must have, or the effect will be vague and unsatisfactory. Now it is number that limits all things; and it is the numerical limitation of the forms of a composition that constitutes rhythm, of which metres are definite sections. Prose, then, is to be rhythmical, but not metrical, or it will become not prose but verse. It should not even have too precise a prose rhythm, and therefore should only be rhythmical to a certain extent.

Of the various rhythms, the heroic has dignity, but lacks the tones of the spoken language. The iambic is the very language of ordinary people, so that in common talk iambic lines occur oftener than any others: but in a speech we need dignity and the power of taking the hearer out of his ordinary self. The trochee is too much akin to wild dancing: we can see this in tetrameter verse, which is one of the trochaic rhythms.

There remains the paean, which speakers began to use in the time of Thrasymachus, though they had then no name to give it. The paean is a third class of rhythm, closely akin to both the two already mentioned; it has in it the ratio of three to two, whereas the other two kinds have the ratio of one to one, and two to one respectively. Between the two last ratios comes the ratio of one-and-a-half to one, which is that of the paean.

Now the other two kinds of rhythm must be rejected in writing prose, partly for the reasons given, and partly because they are too metrical; and the paean must be adopted, since from this alone of the rhythms mentioned no definite metre arises, and therefore it is the least obtrusive of them. At present the same form of paean is employed at the beginning a at the end of sentences, whereas the end should differ from the beginning. There are two opposite kinds of paean, one of which is suitable to the beginning of a sentence, where it is indeed actually used; this is the kind that begins with a long syllable and ends with three short ones, as

"Dalogenes | eite Luki | an, "

and

"Chruseokom | a Ekate | pai Dios. "

The other paean begins, conversely, with three short syllables and ends with a long one, as

"meta de lan | udata t ok | eanon e | oanise nux. "

This kind of paean makes a real close: a short syllable can give no effect of finality, and therefore makes the rhythm appear truncated. A sentence should break off with the long syllable: the fact that it is over should be indicated not by the scribe, or by his period-mark in the margin, but by the rhythm itself.

We have now seen that our language must be rhythmical and not destitute of rhythm, and what rhythms, in what particular shape, make it so.

Part 9

The language of prose must be either free-running, with its parts united by nothing except the connecting words, like the preludes in dithyrambs; or compact and antithetical, like the strophes of the old poets. The free-running style is the ancient one, e.g. 'Herein is set forth the inquiry of Herodotus the Thurian.' Every one used this method formerly; not many do so now. By 'free-running' style I mean the kind that has no natural stopping-places, and comes to a stop only because there is no more to say of that subject. This style is unsatisfying just because it goes on indefinitely-one always likes to sight a stopping-place in front of one: it is only at the goal that men in a race faint and collapse; while they see the end of the course before them, they can keep on going. Such, then, is the free-running kind of style; the compact is that which is in periods. By a period I mean a portion of speech that has in itself a beginning and an end, being at the same time not too big to be taken in at a glance. Language of this kind is satisfying and easy to follow. It is satisfying, because it is just the reverse of indefinite; and moreover, the hearer always feels that he is grasping something and has reached some definite conclusion; whereas it is unsatisfactory to see nothing in front of you and get nowhere. It is easy to follow, because it can easily be remembered; and this because language when in periodic form can be numbered, and number is the easiest of all things to remember. That is why verse, which is measured, is always more easily remembered than prose, which is not: the measures of verse can be numbered. The period must, further, not be completed until the sense is complete: it must not be capable of breaking off abruptly, as may happen with the following iambic lines of Sophocles-

"Calydon's soil is this; of Pelops' land

"(The smiling plains face us across the strait.) "

By a wrong division of the words the hearer may take the meaning to be the reverse of what it is: for instance, in the passage quoted, one might imagine that Calydon is in the Peloponnesus.

A Period may be either divided into several members or simple. The period of several members is a portion of speech (1) complete in itself, (2) divided into parts, and (3) easily delivered at a single breath-as a whole, that is; not by fresh breath being taken at the division. A member is one of the two parts of such a period. By a 'simple' period, I mean that which has only one member. The members, and the whole periods, should be neither curt nor long. A member which is too short often makes the listener stumble; he is still expecting the rhythm to go on to the limit his mind has fixed for it; and if meanwhile he is pulled back by the speaker's stopping, the shock is bound to make him, so to speak, stumble. If, on the other hand, you go on too long, you make him feel left behind, just as people who when walking pass beyond the boundary before turning back leave their companions behind So too if a period is too long you turn it into a speech, or something like a dithyrambic prelude. The result is much like the preludes that Democritus of Chios jeered at Melanippides for writing instead of antistrophic stanzas-

"He that sets traps for another man's feet

"Is like to fall into them first;

"And long-winded preludes do harm to us all,

"But the preluder catches it worst. "

Which applies likewise to long-membered orators. Periods whose members are altogether too short are not periods at all; and the result is to bring the hearer down with a crash.

The periodic style which is divided into members is of two kinds. It is either simply divided, as in 'I have often wondered at the conveners of national gatherings and the founders of athletic contests'; or it is antithetical, where, in each of the two members, one of one pair of opposites is put along with one of another pair, or the same word is used to bracket two opposites, as 'They aided both parties-not only those who stayed behind but those who accompanied them: for the latter they acquired new territory larger than that at home, and to the former they left territory at home that was large enough'. Here the contrasted words are 'staying behind' and 'accompanying', 'enough' and 'larger'. So in the example, 'Both to those who want to get property and to those who desire to enjoy it' where 'enjoyment' is contrasted with 'getting'. Again, 'it often happens in such enterprises that the wise men fail and the fools succeed'; 'they were awarded the prize of valour immediately, and won the command of the sea not long afterwards'; 'to sail through the mainland and march through the sea, by bridging the Hellespont and cutting through Athos'; 'nature gave them their country and law took it away again'; 'of them perished in misery, others were saved in disgrace'; 'Athenian citizens keep foreigners in their houses as servants, while the city of Athens allows her allies by thousands to live as the foreigner's slaves'; and 'to possess in life or to bequeath at death'. There is also what some one said about Peitholaus and Lycophron in a law-court, 'These men used to sell you when they were at home, and now they have come to you here and bought you'. All these passages have the structure described above. Such a form of speech is satisfying, because the significance of contrasted ideas is easily felt, especially when they are thus put side by side, and also because it has the effect of a logical argument; it is by putting two opposing conclusions side by side that you prove one of them false.

Such, then, is the nature of antithesis. Parisosis is making the two members of a period equal in length. Paromoeosis is making the extreme words of both members like each other. This must happen either at the beginning or at the end of each member. If at the beginning, the resemblance must always be between whole words; at the end, between final syllables or inflexions of the same word or the same word repeated. Thus, at the beginning

"agron gar elaben arlon par' autou "

and

"dorhetoi t epelonto pararretoi t epeessin "

At the end

"ouk wethesan auton paidion tetokenai,

"all autou aitlon lelonenai, "

and

"en pleiotals de opontisi kai en elachistais elpisin "

An example of inflexions of the same word is

"axios de staoenai chalkous ouk axios on chalkou; "

Of the same word repeated,

"su d' auton kai zonta eleges kakos kai nun grafeis kakos. "

Of one syllable,

"ti d' an epaoes deinon, ei andrh' eides arhgon; "

It is possible for the same sentence to have all these features together-antithesis, parison, and homoeoteleuton. (The possible beginnings of periods have been pretty fully enumerated in the Theodectea.) There are also spurious antitheses, like that of Epicharmus-

"There one time I as their guest did stay,

"And they were my hosts on another day. "

Part 10

We may now consider the above points settled, and pass on to say something about the way to devise lively and taking sayings. Their actual invention can only come through natural talent or long practice; but this treatise may indicate the way it is done. We may deal with them by enumerating the different kinds of them. We will begin by remarking that we all naturally find it agreeable to get hold of new ideas easily: words express ideas, and therefore those words are the most agreeable that enable us to get hold of new ideas. Now strange words simply puzzle us; ordinary words convey only what we know already; it is from metaphor that we can best get hold of something fresh. When the poet calls 'old age a withered stalk', he conveys a new idea, a new fact, to us by means of the general notion of bloom, which is common to both things. The similes of the poets do the same, and therefore, if they are good similes, give an effect of brilliance. The simile, as has been said before, is a metaphor, differing from it only in the way it is put; and just because it is longer it is less attractive. Besides, it does not say outright that 'this' is 'that', and therefore the hearer is less interested in the idea. We see, then, that both speech and reasoning are lively in proportion as they make us seize a new idea promptly. For this reason people are not much taken either by obvious arguments (using the word 'obvious' to mean what is plain to everybody and needs no investigation), nor by those which puzzle us when we hear them stated, but only by those which convey their information to us as soon as we hear them, provided we had not the information already; or which the mind only just fails to keep up with. These two kinds do convey to us a sort of information: but the obvious and the obscure kinds convey nothing, either at once or later on. It is these qualities, then, that, so far as the meaning of what is said is concerned, make an argument acceptable. So far as the style is concerned, it is the antithetical form that appeals to us, e.g. 'judging that the peace common to all the rest was a war upon their own private interests', where there is an antithesis between war and peace. It is also good to use metaphorical words; but the metaphors must not be far-fetched, or they will be difficult to grasp, nor obvious, or they will have no effect. The words, too, ought to set the scene before our eyes; for events ought to be seen in progress rather than in prospect. So we must aim at these three points: Antithesis, Metaphor, and Actuality.

Of the four kinds of Metaphor the most taking is the proportional kind. Thus Pericles, for instance, said that the vanishing from their country of the young men who had fallen in the war was 'as if the spring were taken out of the year'. Leptines, speaking of the Lacedaemonians, said that he would not have the Athenians let Greece 'lose one of her two eyes'. When Chares was pressing for leave to be examined upon his share in the Olynthiac war, Cephisodotus was indignant, saying that he wanted his examination to take place 'while he had his fingers upon the people's throat'. The same speaker once urged the Athenians to march to Euboea, 'with Miltiades' decree as their rations'. Iphicrates, indignant at the truce made by the Athenians with Epidaurus and the neighbouring sea-board, said that they had stripped themselves of their travelling money for the journey of war. Peitholaus called the state-galley 'the people's big stick', and Sestos 'the corn-bin of the Peiraeus'. Pericles bade his countrymen remove Aegina, 'that eyesore of the Peiraeus.' And Moerocles said he was no more a rascal than was a certain respectable citizen he named, 'whose rascality was worth over thirty per cent per annum to him, instead of a mere ten like his own'.There is also the iambic line of Anaxandrides about the way his daughters put off marrying-

"My daughters' marriage-bonds are overdue. "

Polyeuctus said of a paralytic man named Speusippus that he could not keep quiet, 'though fortune had fastened him in the pillory of disease'. Cephisodotus called warships 'painted millstones'. Diogenes the Dog called taverns 'the mess-rooms of Attica'. Aesion said that the Athenians had 'emptied' their town into Sicily: this is a graphic metaphor. 'Till all Hellas shouted aloud' may be regarded as a metaphor, and a graphic one again. Cephisodotus bade the Athenians take care not to hold too many 'parades'. Isocrates used the same word of those who 'parade at the national festivals.' Another example occurs in the Funeral Speech: 'It is fitting that Greece should cut off her hair beside the tomb of those who fell at Salamis, since her freedom and their valour are buried in the same grave.' Even if the speaker here had only said that it was right to weep when valour was being buried in their grave, it would have been a metaphor, and a graphic one; but the coupling of 'their valour' and 'her freedom' presents a kind of antithesis as well. 'The course of my words', said Iphicrates, 'lies straight through the middle of Chares' deeds': this is a proportional metaphor, and the phrase 'straight through the middle' makes it graphic. The expression 'to call in one danger to rescue us from another' is a graphic metaphor. Lycoleon said, defending Chabrias, 'They did not respect even that bronze statue of his that intercedes for him yonder'.This was a metaphor for the moment, though it would not always apply; a vivid metaphor, however; Chabrias is in danger, and his statue intercedes for him-that lifeless yet living thing which records his services to his country. 'Practising in every way littleness of mind' is metaphorical, for practising a quality implies increasing it. So is 'God kindled our reason to be a lamp within our soul', for both reason and light reveal things. So is 'we are not putting an end to our wars, but only postponing them', for both literal postponement and the making of such a peace as this apply to future action. So is such a saying as 'This treaty is a far nobler trophy than those we set up on fields of battle; they celebrate small gains and single successes; it celebrates our triumph in the war as a whole'; for both trophy and treaty are signs of victory. So is 'A country pays a heavy reckoning in being condemned by the judgement of mankind', for a reckoning is damage deservedly incurred.

Part 11

It has already been mentioned that liveliness is got by using the proportional type of metaphor and being making (ie. making your hearers see things). We have still to explain what we mean by their 'seeing things', and what must be done to effect this. By 'making them see things' I mean using expressions that represent things as in a state of activity. Thus, to say that a good man is 'four-square' is certainly a metaphor; both the good man and the square are perfect; but the metaphor does not suggest activity. On the other hand, in the expression 'with his vigour in full bloom' there is a notion of activity; and so in 'But you must roam as free as a sacred victim'; and in

"Thereas up sprang the Hellenes to their feet, "

where 'up sprang' gives us activity as well as metaphor, for it at once suggests swiftness. So with Homer's common practice of giving metaphorical life to lifeless things: all such passages are distinguished by the effect of activity they convey. Thus,

"Downward anon to the valley rebounded the boulder remorseless; and "

"The (bitter) arrow flew; "

and

"Flying on eagerly; and "

Stuck in the earth, still panting to feed on the flesh of the heroes; and

"And the point of the spear in its fury drove

"full through his breastbone. "

In all these examples the things have the effect of being active because they are made into living beings; shameless behaviour and fury and so on are all forms of activity. And the poet has attached these ideas to the things by means of proportional metaphors: as the stone is to Sisyphus, so is the shameless man to his victim. In his famous similes, too, he treats inanimate things in the same way:

"Curving and crested with white, host following

"host without ceasing. "

Here he represents everything as moving and living; and activity is movement.

Metaphors must be drawn, as has been said already, from things that are related to the original thing, and yet not obviously so related-just as in philosophy also an acute mind will perceive resemblances even in things far apart. Thus Archytas said that an arbitrator and an altar were the same, since the injured fly to both for refuge. Or you might say that an anchor and an overhead hook were the same, since both are in a way the same, only the one secures things from below and the other from above. And to speak of states as 'levelled' is to identify two widely different things, the equality of a physical surface and the equality of political powers.

Liveliness is specially conveyed by metaphor, and by the further power of surprising the hearer; because the hearer expected something different, his acquisition of the new idea impresses him all the more. His mind seems to say, 'Yes, to be sure; I never thought of that'. The liveliness of epigrammatic remarks is due to the meaning not being just what the words say: as in the saying of Stesichorus that 'the cicalas will chirp to themselves on the ground'. Well-constructed riddles are attractive for the same reason; a new idea is conveyed, and there is metaphorical expression. So with the 'novelties' of Theodorus. In these the thought is startling, and, as Theodorus puts it, does not fit in with the ideas you already have. They are like the burlesque words that one finds in the comic writers. The effect is produced even by jokes depending upon changes of the letters of a word; this too is a surprise. You find this in verse as well as in prose. The word which comes is not what the hearer imagined: thus

"Onward he came, and his feet were shod with his-chilblains, "

where one imagined the word would be 'sandals'. But the point should be clear the moment the words are uttered. Jokes made by altering the letters of a word consist in meaning, not just what you say, but something that gives a twist to the word used; e.g. the remark of Theodorus about Nicon the harpist Thratt' ei su ('you Thracian slavey'), where he pretends to mean Thratteis su ('you harpplayer'), and surprises us when we find he means something else. So you enjoy the point when you see it, though the remark will fall flat unless you are aware that Nicon is Thracian. Or again: Boulei auton persai. In both these cases the saying must fit the facts. This is also true of such lively remarks as the one to the effect that to the Athenians their empire (arche) of the sea was not the beginning (arche) of their troubles, since they gained by it. Or the opposite one of Isocrates, that their empire (arche) was the beginning (arche) of their troubles. Either way, the speaker says something unexpected, the soundness of which is thereupon recognized. There would be nothing clever is saying 'empire is empire'. Isocrates means more than that, and uses the word with a new meaning. So too with the former saying, which denies that arche in one sense was arche in another sense. In all these jokes, whether a word is used in a second sense or metaphorically, the joke is good if it fits the facts. For instance, Anaschetos (proper name) ouk anaschetos: where you say that what is so-and-so in one sense is not so-and-so in another; well, if the man is unpleasant, the joke fits the facts. Again, take-

"Thou must not be a stranger stranger than Thou should'st. "

Do not the words 'thou must not be', &c., amount to saying that the stranger must not always be strange? Here again is the use of one word in different senses. Of the same kind also is the much-praised verse of Anaxandrides:

"Death is most fit before you do

"Deeds that would make death fit for you. "

This amounts to saying 'it is a fit thing to die when you are not fit to die', or 'it is a fit thing to die when death is not fit for you', i.e. when death is not the fit return for what you are doing. The type of language employed-is the same in all these examples; but the more briefly and antithetically such sayings can be expressed, the more taking they are, for antithesis impresses the new idea more firmly and brevity more quickly. They should always have either some personal application or some merit of expression, if they are to be true without being commonplace-two requirements not always satisfied simultaneously. Thus 'a man should die having done no wrong' is true but dull: 'the right man should marry the right woman' is also true but dull. No, there must be both good qualities together, as in 'it is fitting to die when you are not fit for death'. The more a saying has these qualitis, the livelier it appears: if, for instance, its wording is metaphorical, metaphorical in the right way, antithetical, and balanced, and at the same time it gives an idea of activity.

Successful similes also, as has been said above, are in a sense metaphors, since they always involve two relations like the proportional metaphor. Thus: a shield, we say, is the 'drinking-bowl of Ares', and a bow is the 'chordless lyre'. This way of putting a metaphor is not 'simple', as it would be if we called the bow a lyre or the shield a drinking-bowl. There are 'simple' similes also: we may say that a flute-player is like a monkey, or that a short-sighted man's eyes are like a lamp-flame with water dropping on it, since both eyes and flame keep winking. A simile succeeds best when it is a converted metaphor, for it is possible to say that a shield is like the drinking-bowl of Ares, or that a ruin is like a house in rags, and to say that Niceratus is like a Philoctetes stung by Pratys-the simile made by Thrasyniachus when he saw Niceratus, who had been beaten by Pratys in a recitation competition, still going about unkempt and unwashed. It is in these respects that poets fail worst when they fail, and succeed best when they succeed, i.e. when they give the resemblance pat, as in

"Those legs of his curl just like parsley leaves; "

and

"Just like Philammon struggling with his punchball. "

These are all similes; and that similes are metaphors has been stated often already.

Proverbs, again, are metaphors from one species to another. Suppose, for instance, a man to start some undertaking in hope of gain and then to lose by it later on, 'Here we have once more the man of Carpathus and his hare', says he. For both alike went through the said experience.

It has now been explained fairly completely how liveliness is secured and why it has the effect it has. Successful hyperboles are also metaphors, e.g. the one about the man with a black eye, 'you would have thought he was a basket of mulberries'; here the 'black eye' is compared to a mulberry because of its colour, the exaggeration lying in the quantity of mulberries suggested. The phrase 'like so-and-so' may introduce a hyperbole under the form of a simile. Thus

"Just like Philammon struggling with his punchball "

is equivalent to 'you would have thought he was Philammon struggling with his punchball'; and

"Those legs of his curl just like parsley leaves "

is equivalent to 'his legs are so curly that you would have thought they were not legs but parsley leaves'. Hyperboles are for young men to use; they show vehemence of character; and this is why angry people use them more than other people.

"Not though he gave me as much as the dust

"or the sands of the sea...

"But her, the daughter of Atreus' son, I never will marry,

"Nay, not though she were fairer than Aphrodite the Golden,

"Defter of hand than Athene... "

(The Attic orators are particularly fond of this method of speech.) Consequently it does not suit an elderly speaker.

Part 12

It should be observed that each kind of rhetoric has its own appropriate style. The style of written prose is not that of spoken oratory, nor are those of political and forensic speaking the same. Both written and spoken have to be known. To know the latter is to know how to speak good Greek. To know the former means that you are not obliged, as otherwise you are, to hold your tongue when you wish to communicate something to the general public.

The written style is the more finished: the spoken better admits of dramatic delivery-like the kind of oratory that reflects character and the kind that reflects emotion. Hence actors look out for plays written in the latter style, and poets for actors competent to act in such plays. Yet poets whose plays are meant to be read are read and circulated: Chaeremon, for instance, who is as finished as a professional speech-writer; and Licymnius among the dithyrambic poets. Compared with those of others, the speeches of professional writers sound thin in actual contests. Those of the orators, on the other hand, are good to hear spoken, but look amateurish enough when they pass into the hands of a reader. This is just because they are so well suited for an actual tussle, and therefore contain many dramatic touches, which, being robbed of all dramatic rendering, fail to do their own proper work, and consequently look silly. Thus strings of unconnected words, and constant repetitions of words and phrases, are very properly condemned in written speeches: but not in spoken speeches-speakers use them freely, for they have a dramatic effect. In this repetition there must be variety of tone, paving the way, as it were, to dramatic effect; e.g. 'This is the villain among you who deceived you, who cheated you, who meant to betray you completely'. This is the sort of thing that Philemon the actor used to do in the Old Men's Madness of Anaxandrides whenever he spoke the words 'Rhadamanthus and Palamedes', and also in the prologue to the Saints whenever he pronounced the pronoun 'I'. If one does not deliver such things cleverly, it becomes a case of 'the man who swallowed a poker'. So too with strings of unconnected words, e.g.'I came to him; I met him; I besought him'. Such passages must be acted, not delivered with the same quality and pitch of voice, as though they had only one idea in them. They have the further peculiarity of suggesting that a number of separate statements have been made in the time usually occupied by one. Just as the use of conjunctions makes many statements into a single one, so the omission of conjunctions acts in the reverse way and makes a single one into many. It thus makes everything more important: e.g. 'I came to him; I talked to him; I entreated him'-what a lot of facts! the hearer thinks-'he paid no attention to anything I said'. This is the effect which Homer seeks when he writes,

"Nireus likewise from Syme (three well-fashioned ships did bring),

"Nireus, the son of Aglaia (and Charopus, bright-faced king),

"Nireus, the comeliest man (of all that to Ilium's strand). "

If many things are said about a man, his name must be mentioned many times; and therefore people think that, if his name is mentioned many times, many things have been said about him. So that Homer, by means of this illusion, has made a great deal of though he has mentioned him only in this one passage, and has preserved his memory, though he nowhere says a word about him afterwards.

Now the style of oratory addressed to public assemblies is really just like scene-painting. The bigger the throng, the more distant is the point of view: so that, in the one and the other, high finish in detail is superfluous and seems better away. The forensic style is more highly finished; still more so is the style of language addressed to a single judge, with whom there is very little room for rhetorical artifices, since he can take the whole thing in better, and judge of what is to the point and what is not; the struggle is less intense and so the judgement is undisturbed. This is why the same speakers do not distinguish themselves in all these branches at once; high finish is wanted least where dramatic delivery is wanted most, and here the speaker must have a good voice, and above all, a strong one. It is ceremonial oratory that is most literary, for it is meant to be read; and next to it forensic oratory.

To analyse style still further, and add that it must be agreeable or magnificent, is useless; for why should it have these traits any more than 'restraint', 'liberality', or any other moral excellence? Obviously agreeableness will be produced by the qualities already mentioned, if our definition of excellence of style has been correct. For what other reason should style be 'clear', and 'not mean' but 'appropriate'? If it is prolix, it is not clear; nor yet if it is curt. Plainly the middle way suits best. Again, style will be made agreeable by the elements mentioned, namely by a good blending of ordinary and unusual words, by the rhythm, and by-the persuasiveness that springs from appropriateness.

This concludes our discussion of style, both in its general aspects and in its special applications to the various branches of rhetoric. We have now to deal with Arrangement.

Part 13

A speech has two parts. You must state your case, and you must prove it. You cannot either state your case and omit to prove it, or prove it without having first stated it; since any proof must be a proof of something, and the only use of a preliminary statement is the proof that follows it. Of these two parts the first part is called the Statement of the case, the second part the Argument, just as we distinguish between Enunciation and Demonstration. The current division is absurd. For 'narration' surely is part of a forensic speech only: how in a political speech or a speech of display can there be 'narration' in the technical sense? or a reply to a forensic opponent? or an epilogue in closely-reasoned speeches? Again, introduction, comparison of conflicting arguments, and recapitulation are only found in political speeches when there is a struggle between two policies. They may occur then; so may even accusation and defence, often enough; but they form no essential part of a political speech. Even forensic speeches do not always need epilogues; not, for instance, a short speech, nor one in which the facts are easy to remember, the effect of an epilogue being always a reduction in the apparent length. It follows, then, that the only necessary parts of a speech are the Statement and the Argument. These are the essential features of a speech; and it cannot in any case have more than Introduction, Statement, Argument, and Epilogue. 'Refutation of the Opponent' is part of the arguments: so is 'Comparison' of the opponent's case with your own, for that process is a magnifying of your own case and therefore a part of the arguments, since one who does this proves something. The Introduction does nothing like this; nor does the Epilogue-it merely reminds us of what has been said already. If we make such distinctions we shall end, like Theodorus and his followers, by distinguishing 'narration' proper from 'post-narration' and 'pre-narration', and 'refutation' from 'final refutation'. But we ought only to bring in a new name if it indicates a real species with distinct specific qualities; otherwise the practice is pointless and silly, like the way Licymnius invented names in his Art of Rhetoric-'Secundation', 'Divagation', 'Ramification'.

Part 14

The Introduction is the beginning of a speech, corresponding to the prologue in poetry and the prelude in flute-music; they are all beginnings, paving the way, as it were, for what is to follow. The musical prelude resembles the introduction to speeches of display; as flute players play first some brilliant passage they know well and then fit it on to the opening notes of the piece itself, so in speeches of display the writer should proceed in the same way; he should begin with what best takes his fancy, and then strike up his theme and lead into it; which is indeed what is always done. (Take as an example the introduction to the Helen of Isocrates-there is nothing in common between the 'eristics' and Helen.) And here, even if you travel far from your subject, it is fitting, rather than that there should be sameness in the entire speech.

The usual subject for the introductions to speeches of display is some piece of praise or censure. Thus Gorgias writes in his Olympic Speech, 'You deserve widespread admiration, men of Greece', praising thus those who start,ed the festival gatherings.' Isocrates, on the other hand, censures them for awarding distinctions to fine athletes but giving no prize for intellectual ability. Or one may begin with a piece of advice, thus: 'We ought to honour good men and so I myself am praising Aristeides' or 'We ought to honour those who are unpopular but not bad men, men whose good qualities have never been noticed, like Alexander son of Priam.' Here the orator gives advice. Or we may begin as speakers do in the law-courts; that is to say, with appeals to the audience to excuse us if our speech is about something paradoxical, difficult, or hackneyed; like Choerilus in the lines-

"But now when allotment of all has been made... "

Introductions to speeches of display, then, may be composed of some piece of praise or censure, of advice to do or not to do something, or of appeals to the audience; and you must choose between making these preliminary passages connected or disconnected with the speech itself.

Introductions to forensic speeches, it must be observed, have the same value as the prologues of dramas and the introductions to epic poems; the dithyrambic prelude resembling the introduction to a speech of display, as

"For thee, and thy gilts, and thy battle-spoils.... "

In prologues, and in epic poetry, a foretaste of the theme is given, intended to inform the hearers of it in advance instead of keeping their minds in suspense. Anything vague puzzles them: so give them a grasp of the beginning, and they can hold fast to it and follow the argument. So we find-

"Sing, O goddess of song, of the Wrath...

"Tell me, O Muse, of the hero...

"Lead me to tell a new tale, how there came great warfare to Europe

"Out of the Asian land... "

The tragic poets, too, let us know the pivot of their play; if not at the outset like Euripides, at least somewhere in the preface to a speech like Sophocles-

"Polybus was my father...; "

and so in Comedy. This, then, is the most essential function and distinctive property of the introduction, to show what the aim of the speech is; and therefore no introduction ought to be employed where the subject is not long or intricate.

The other kinds of introduction employed are remedial in purpose, and may be used in any type of speech. They are concerned with the speaker, the hearer, the subject, or the speaker's opponent. Those concerned with the speaker himself or with his opponent are directed to removing or exciting prejudice. But whereas the defendant will begin by dealing with this sort of thing, the prosecutor will take quite another line and deal with such matters in the closing part of his speech. The reason for this is not far to seek. The defendant, when he is going to bring himself on the stage, must clear away any obstacles, and therefore must begin by removing any prejudice felt against him. But if you are to excite prejudice, you must do so at the close, so that the judges may more easily remember what you have said.

The appeal to the hearer aims at securing his goodwill, or at arousing his resentment, or sometimes at gaining his serious attention to the case, or even at distracting it-for gaining it is not always an advantage, and speakers will often for that reason try to make him laugh.

You may use any means you choose to make your hearer receptive; among others, giving him a good impression of your character, which always helps to secure his attention. He will be ready to attend to anything that touches himself and to anything that is important, surprising, or agreeable; and you should accordingly convey to him the impression that what you have to say is of this nature. If you wish to distract his attention, you should imply that the subject does not affect him, or is trivial or disagreeable. But observe, all this has nothing to do with the speech itself. It merely has to do with the weak-minded tendency of the hearer to listen to what is beside the point. Where this tendency is absent, no introduction wanted beyond a summary statement of your subject, to put a sort of head on the main body of your speech. Moreover, calls for attention, when required, may come equally well in any part of a speech; in fact, the beginning of it is just where there is least slackness of interest; it is therefore ridiculous to put this kind of thing at the beginning, when every one is listening with most attention. Choose therefore any point in the speech where such an appeal is needed, and then say 'Now I beg you to note this point-it concerns you quite as much as myself'; or

"I will tell you that whose like you have never yet "

heard for terror, or for wonder. This is what Prodicus called 'slipping in a bit of the fifty-drachma show-lecture for the audience whenever they began to nod'. It is plain that such introductions are addressed not to ideal hearers, but to hearers as we find them. The use of introductions to excite prejudice or to dispel misgivings is universal-

"My lord, I will not say that eagerly... "

or

"Why all this preface? "

Introductions are popular with those whose case is weak, or looks weak; it pays them to dwell on anything rather than the actual facts of it. That is why slaves, instead of answering the questions put to them, make indirect replies with long preambles. The means of exciting in your hearers goodwill and various other feelings of the same kind have already been described. The poet finely says May I find in Phaeacian hearts, at my coming, goodwill and compassion; and these are the two things we should aim at. In speeches of display we must make the hearer feel that the eulogy includes either himself or his family or his way of life or something or other of the kind. For it is true, as Socrates says in the Funeral Speech, that 'the difficulty is not to praise the Athenians at Athens but at Sparta'.

The introductions of political oratory will be made out of the same materials as those of the forensic kind, though the nature of political oratory makes them very rare. The subject is known already, and therefore the facts of the case need no introduction; but you may have to say something on account of yourself or to your opponents; or those present may be inclined to treat the matter either more or less seriously than you wish them to. You may accordingly have to excite or dispel some prejudice, or to make the matter under discussion seem more or less important than before: for either of which purposes you will want an introduction. You may also want one to add elegance to your remarks, feeling that otherwise they will have a casual air, like Gorgias' eulogy of the Eleans, in which, without any preliminary sparring or fencing, he begins straight off with 'Happy city of Elis!'

Part 15

One way of removing prejudice is to make use of the arguments by which one may clear oneself from disagreeable suspicion; for it makes no difference whether this suspicion has been openly expressed or not; and so this may be taken as a general rule.
[2] Another way[1] consists in contesting the disputed points, either by denying the fact or its harmfulness, at least to the plaintiff; or by asserting that its importance is exaggerated; or that it is not unjust at all, or only slightly so; or neither disgraceful nor important. These are the possible points of dispute: as Iphicrates, in answer to Nausicrates, admitted that he had done what the prosecutor alleged and inflicted damage, but denied that he had been guilty of wrongdoing. Again, one may strike the balance, when guilty of wrongdoing, by maintaining that although the action was injurious it was honorable, painful but useful, or anything else of the

kind.

[3] Another method consists in saying that it was a case of error, misfortune, or necessity; as, for example, Sophocles said that he trembled, not, as the accuser said, in order to appear old, but from necessity, for it was against his wish that he was eighty years of age.[1] One may also substitute one motive for another, and say that one did not mean to injure but to do something else, not that of which one was accused, and that the wrongdoing was accidental: "I should deserve your hatred, had I acted so as to bring this about."

[4] Another method may be employed if the accuser, either himself or one closely related to him, has been involved in a similar charge, either now or formerly;

[5] or, if others are involved who are admittedly not exposed to the charge; for instance, if it is argued that so-and-so is an adulterer, because he is a dandy, then so-and-so must be.

[6] Again, if the accuser has already similarly accused others, or himself been accused by others; or if others, without being formally accused, have been suspected as you are now, and their innocence has been proved.

[7] Another method consists in counter-attacking the accuser; for it would be absurd to believe the words of one who is himself unworthy of belief.

[8] Another method is to appeal to a verdict already given, as Euripides did in the case about the exchange of property; when Hygiaenon accused him of impiety as having advised perjury in the verse, " My tongue hath sworn, but my mind is unsworn,

" Euripides replied that his accuser did wrong in transferring the decisions of the court of Dionysus to the law courts; for he had already rendered an account of what he had said there, or was still ready to do so, if his adversary desired to accuse him.

[9] Another method consists in attacking slander, showing how great an evil it is, and this because it alters the nature of judgements, and that it does not rely on the real facts of the case.

Common to both parties is the topic of tokens, as in the Teucer, Odysseus reproaches Teucer with being a relative of Priam, whose sister his mother Hesione was; to which Teucer replied that his father Telamon was the enemy of Priam, and that he himself did not denounce the spies.

[10] Another method, suitable for the accuser, is to praise something unimportant at great length, and to condemn something important concisely; or, putting forward several things that are praiseworthy in the opponent, to condemn the one thing that has an important bearing upon the case. Such methods are most artful and unfair; for by their use men endeavor to make what is good in a man injurious to him, by mixing it up with what is bad.

Another method is common to both accuser and defender. Since the same thing may have been done from several motives, the accuser must disparage it by taking it in the worse sense, while the defender must take it in the better sense. For instance, when Diomedes chose Odysseus for his companion, it may be said on the one hand that he did so because he considered him to be the bravest of men, on the other, that it was because Odysseus was the only man who was no possible rival for him, since he was a poltroon. Let this suffice for the question of prejudice.

Part 16

In the epideictic style the narrative should not be consecutive, but disjointed; for it is necessary to go through the actions which form the subject of the speech. For a speech is made up of one part that is inartificial (the speaker being in no way the author of the actions which he relates), and of another that does depend upon art. The latter consists in showing that the action did take place, if it be incredible, or that it is of a certain kind, or of a certain importance, or all three together.

[2] This is why it is sometimes right not to narrate all the facts consecutively, because a demonstration of this kind is difficult to remember. From some facts a man may be shown to be courageous, from others wise or just. Besides, a speech of this kind is simpler, whereas the other is intricate and not plain.

[3] It is only necessary to recall famous actions; wherefore most people have no need of narrative—for instance, if you wish to praise Achilles; for everybody knows what he did, and it is only necessary to make use of it. But if you wish to praise Critias, narrative is necessary, for not many people know what he did . . .

[4] But at the present day it is absurdly laid down that the narrative should be rapid. And yet, as the man said to the baker when he asked whether he was to knead bread hard or soft, "What! is it impossible to knead it well?" so it is in this case; for the narrative must not be long, nor the exordium, nor the proofs either. For in this case also propriety does not consist either in rapidity or conciseness, but in a due mean; that is, one must say all that will make the facts clear, or create the belief that they have happened or have done injury or wrong, or that they are as important as you wish to make them. The opposite party must do the opposite.

[5] And you should incidentally narrate anything that tends to show your own virtue, for instance, "I always recommended him to act rightly, not to forsake his children"; or the wickedness of your opponent, for instance, "but he answered that, wherever he might be, he would always find other children," an answer attributed by Herodotus[1] to the Egyptian rebels; or anything which is likely to please the dicasts.

1 **Hdt. 2.30**. The story was that a number of Egyptian soldiers had revolted and left in a body for Ethiopia. Their king Psammetichus begged them not to desert their wives and children, to which one of them made answer

[6] In defence, the narrative need not be so long; for the points at issue are either that the fact has not happened or that it was neither injurious nor wrong nor so important as asserted, so that one should not waste time over what all are agreed upon, unless anything tends to prove that, admitting the act, it is not wrong.

[7] Again, one should only mention such past things as are likely to excite pity or indignation if described as actually happening; for instance, the story of Alcinous, because in the presence of Penelope it is reduced to sixty lines, and the way in which Phayllus dealt with the epic cycle, and the prologue to the Oeneus.

[8] And the narrative should be of a moral character, and in fact it will be so, if we know what effects this. One thing is to make clear our moral purpose; for as is the moral purpose, so is the character, and as is the end, so is the moral purpose. For this reason mathematical treatises have no moral character, because neither have they moral purpose; for they have no moral end. But

the Socratic dialogues have; for they discuss such questions.

[9] Other ethical indications are the accompanying peculiarities of each individual character; for instance, "He was talking and walking on at the same time," which indicates effrontery and boorishness. Nor should we speak as if from the intellect, after the manner of present-day orators; but from moral purpose: "But I wished it, and I preferred it; and even if I profited nothing, it is better." The first statement indicates prudence, the second virtue; for prudence consists in the pursuit of what is useful, virtue in that of what is honorable. If anything of the kind seems incredible, then the reason must be added; of this Sophocles gives an example, where his Antigone says that she cared more for her brother than for her husband or children; for the latter can be replaced after they are gone, " but when father and mother are in the grave, no brother can ever be born.

" If you have no reason, you should at least say that you are aware that what you assert is incredible, but that it is your nature; for no one believes that a man ever does anything of his own free will except from motives of self-interest.

[10] Further, the narrative should draw upon what is emotional by the introduction of such of its accompaniments as are well known, and of what is specially characteristic of either yourself or of the adversary: "And he went off looking grimly at me";
and as Aeschines says of Cratylus, that he hissed violently and violently shook his fists. Such details produce persuasion because, being known to the hearer, they become tokens of what he does not know. Numerous examples of this may be found in Homer: " Thus she spoke, and the aged nurse covered her face with her hands;

" for those who are beginning to weep lay hold on their eyes. And you should at once introduce yourself and your adversary as being of a certain character, that the hearers may regard you or him as such; but do not let it be seen. That this is easy is perfectly clear from the example of messengers; we do not yet know what they are going to say, but nevertheless we have an inkling of it.

[11] Again, the narrative should be introduced in several places, sometimes not at all at the beginning. In deliberative oratory narrative is very rare, because no one can narrate things to come; but if there is narrative, it will be of things past, in order that, being reminded of them, the hearers may take better counsel about the future. This may be done in a spirit either of blame or of praise; but in that case the speaker does not perform the function of the deliberative orator. If there is anything incredible, you should immediately promise both to give a reason for it at once and to submit it to the judgement of any whom the hearers approve; as, for instance, Jocasta in the Oedipus of Carcinus is always promising, when the man who is looking for her son makes inquiries
of her; and similarly Haemon in Sophocles.

Part 17

Proofs should be demonstrative, and as the disputed points are four, the demonstration should bear upon the particular point disputed; for instance, if the fact is disputed, proof of this must be brought at the trial before anything else; or if it is maintained that no injury has been done; or that the act was not so important as asserted; or was just, then this must be proved, the three last questions being matters of dispute just as the question of fact.

[2] But do not forget that it is only in the case of a dispute as to this question of fact that one of the two parties must necessarily be a rogue; for ignorance is not the cause, as it might be if a question of right or wrong were the issue; so that in this case one should spend time on this topic, but not in the others.

[3] In epideictic speeches, amplification is employed, as a rule, to prove that things are honorable or useful; for the facts must be taken on trust, since proofs of these are rarely given, and only if they are incredible or the responsibility is attributed to another.

[4] In deliberative oratory, it may be maintained either that certain consequences will not happen, or that what the adversary recommends will happen, but that it will be unjust, inexpedient, or not so important as supposed. But one must also look to see whether he makes any false statements as to things outside the issue; for these look like evidence that he makes misstatements about the issue itself as well.

[5] Examples are best suited to deliberative oratory and enthymemes to forensic. The first is concerned with the future, so that its examples must be derived from the past; the second with the question of the existence or non-existence of facts, in which demonstrative and necessary proofs are more in place; for the past involves a kind of necessity.

[6] One should not introduce a series of enthymemes continuously but mix them up; otherwise they destroy one another. For there is a limit of quantity; thus, " Friend, since thou hast said as much as a wise man would say,

[7] where Homer does not say τοιαῦτα (such things as), but τόσα (as many things as). Nor should you try to find enthymemes about everything; otherwise you will be imitating certain philosophers, who draw conclusions that are better known and more plausible than the premises from which they are drawn.

[8] And whenever you wish to arouse emotion, do not use an enthymeme, for it will either drive out the emotion or it will be useless; for simultaneous movements drive each other out, the result being their mutual destruction or weakening. Nor should you look for an enthymeme at the time when you wish to give the speech an ethical character; for demonstration involves neither moral character nor moral purpose.

[9] Moral maxims, on the other hand, should be used in both narrative and proof; for they express moral character; for instance, "I gave him the money and that although I knew that one ought not to trust." Or, to arouse emotion: "I do not regret it, although I have been wronged; his is the profit, mine the right."

[10] Deliberative speaking is more difficult than forensic, and naturally so, because it has to do with the future; whereas forensic speaking has to do with the past, which is already known, even by diviners, as Epimenides the Cretan said; for he used to divine, not the future, but only things that were past but obscure. Further, the law is the subject in forensic speaking; and when one has a starting-point, it is easier to find a demonstrative proof. Deliberative speaking does not allow many opportunities for lingering—for instance, attacks on the adversary, remarks about oneself, or attempts to arouse emotion. In this branch of Rhetoric there is less room for these than in any other, unless the speaker wanders from the subject. Therefore, when at a loss for topics, one must do as the orators at Athens, amongst them Isocrates, for even when deliberating, he brings

accusations against the Lacedaemonians, for instance, in the <u>Panegyricus</u>, and against Chares in the <u>Symmachikos</u> (On the Peace).

[11] Epideictic speeches should be varied with laudatory episodes, after the manner of Isocrates, who is always bringing somebody in. This is what Gorgias meant when he said that he was never at a loss for something to say; for, if he is speaking of Peleus, he praises Achilles, then Aeacus, then the god; similarly courage, which does this and that, or is of such a kind.

[12] If you have proofs, then, your language must be both ethical and demonstrative; if you have no enthymemes, ethical only. In fact, it is more fitting that a virtuous man should show himself good than that his speech should be painfully exact.

[13] Refutative enthymemes are more popular than demonstrative, because, in all cases of refutation, it is clearer that a logical conclusion has been reached; for opposites are more noticeable when placed in juxtaposition.

[14] The refutation of the opponent is not a particular kind of proof; his arguments should be refuted partly by objection, partly by counter-syllogism. In both deliberative and forensic rhetoric he who speaks first should state his own proofs and afterwards meet the arguments of the opponent, refuting or pulling them to pieces beforehand. But if the opposition is varied, these arguments should be dealt with first, as Callistratus did in the Messenian assembly; in fact, it was only after he had first refuted what his opponents were likely to say that he put forward his own proofs.

[15] He who replies should first state the arguments against the opponent's speech, refuting and answering it by syllogisms, especially if his arguments have met with approval. For as the mind is ill-disposed towards one against whom prejudices have been raised beforehand, it is equally so towards a speech, if the adversary is thought to have spoken well. One must therefore make room in the hearer's mind for the speech one intends to make; and for this purpose you must destroy the impression made by the adversary. Wherefore it is only after having combated all the arguments, or the most important, or those which are plausible, or most easy to refute, that you should substantiate your own case:

" I will first defend the goddesses, for I [do not think] that Hera . . .

" in this passage the poet has first seized upon the weakest argument.

[16] So much concerning proofs. In regard to moral character, since sometimes, in speaking of ourselves, we render ourselves liable to envy, to the charge of prolixity, or contradiction, or, when speaking of another, we may be accused of abuse or boorishness, we must make another speak in our place, as Isocrates does in the <u>Philippus</u> and in the <u>Antidosis</u>. Archilochus uses the same device in censure; for in his iambics he introduces the father speaking as follows of his daughter: " There is nothing beyond expectation, nothing that can be sworn impossible,

" and the carpenter Charon in the iambic verse beginning " I [care not for the wealth] of Gyges;

" Sophocles, also, introduces Haemon, when defending Antigone against his father, as if quoting the opinion of others.

[17] One should also sometimes change enthymemes into moral maxims; for instance, "Sensible men should become reconciled when they are prosperous; for in this manner they will obtain the greatest advantages," which is equivalent to the enthymeme "If men should become reconciled whenever it is most useful and advantageous, they should be reconciled in a time of prosperity."

Part 18

In regard to interrogation, its employment is especially opportune, when the opponent has already stated the opposite, so that the addition of a question makes the result an absurdity; as, for instance, when Pericles interrogated Lampon about initiation into the sacred rites of the savior goddess. On Lampon replying that it was not possible for one who was not initiated to be told about them, Pericles asked him if he himself was acquainted with the rites, and when he said yes, Pericles further asked, "How can that be, seeing that you are uninitiated?"

[2] Again, interrogation should be employed when one of the two propositions is evident, and it is obvious that the opponent will admit the other if you ask him. But the interrogator, having obtained the second premise by putting a question, should not make an additional question of what is evident, but should state the conclusion. For instance, Socrates, when accused by Meletus of not believing in the gods, asked[1] whether he did not say that there was a divine something; and when Meletus said yes, Socrates went on to ask if divine beings were not either children of the gods or something godlike. When Meletus again said yes, Socrates rejoined,

[3] "Is there a man, then, who can admit that the children of the gods exist without at the same time admitting that the gods exist?" Thirdly, when it is intended to show that the opponent either contradicts himself or puts forward a paradox.

[4] Further, when the opponent can do nothing else but answer the question by a sophistical solution; for if he answers, "Partly yes, and partly no," "Some are, but some are not," "In one sense it is so, in another not," the hearers cry out against him as being in a difficulty. In other cases interrogation should not be attempted; for if the adversary raises an objection, the interrogator seems to be defeated; for it is impossible to ask a number of questions, owing to the hearer's weakness. Wherefore also we should compress our enthymemes as much as possible.

[5] Ambiguous questions should be answered by defining them by a regular explanation, and not too concisely; those that appear likely to make us contradict ourselves should be solved at once in the answer, before the adversary has time to ask the next question or to draw a conclusion; for it is not difficult to see the drift of his argument. Both this, however, and the means of answering will be sufficiently clear from the Topics.

[6] If a conclusion is put in the form of a question, we should state the reason for our answer. For instance, Sophocles being asked by Pisander whether he, like the rest of the Committee of Ten,

had approved the setting up of the Four Hundred, he admitted it. "What then?" asked Pisander, "did not this appear to you to be a wicked thing?" Sophocles admitted it. "So then you did what was wicked?" "Yes, for there was nothing better to be done." The Lacedaemonian, who was called to account for his ephoralty, being asked if he did not think that the rest of his colleagues had been justly put to death, answered yes. "But did not you pass the same measures as they did?" "Yes." "Would not you, then, also be justly put to death?" "No; for my colleagues did this for money; I did not, but acted according to my conscience." For this reason we should not ask any further questions after drawing the conclusion, nor put the conclusion itself as a question, unless the balance of truth is unmistakably in our favor.

[7] As for jests, since they may sometimes be useful in debates, the advice of Gorgias was good—to confound the opponents' earnest with jest and their jest with earnest. We have stated in the Poetics how many kinds of jests there are, some of them becoming a gentleman, others not. You should therefore choose the kind that suits you. Irony is more gentlemanly than buffoonery; for the first is employed on one's own account, the second on that of another.

Part 19

The epilogue is composed of four parts: to dispose the hearer favorably towards oneself and unfavorably towards the adversary; to amplify and depreciate; to excite the emotions of the hearer; to recapitulate. For after you have proved that you are truthful and that the adversary is false, the natural order of things is to praise ourselves, blame him, and put the finishing touches. One of two things should be aimed at, to show that you are either relatively or absolutely good and the adversary either relatively or absolutely bad. The topics which serve to represent men as good or bad have already been stated.

[2] After this, when the proof has once been established, the natural thing is to amplify or depreciate; for it is necessary that the facts should be admitted, if it is intended to deal with the question of degree; just as the growth of the body is due to things previously existing. The topics of amplification and depreciation have been previously set forth.

[3] Next, when the nature and importance of the facts are clear, one should rouse the hearer to certain emotions—pity, indignation, anger, hate, jealousy, emulation, and quarrelsomeness. The topics of these also have been previously stated,

[4] so that all that remains is to recapitulate what has been said. This may appropriately be done at this stage in the way certain rhetoricians wrongly recommend for the exordium, when they advise frequent repetition of the points, so that they may be easily learnt. In the exordium we should state the subject, in order that the question to be decided may not escape notice, but in the epilogue we should give a summary statement of the proofs.

[5] We should begin by saying that we have kept our promise, and then state what we have said and why. Our case may also be closely compared with our opponent's; and we may either

compare what both of us have said on the same point, or without direct comparison: "My opponent said so-and-so, and I said so-and-so on this point and for these reasons." Or ironically, as for instance, "He said this and I answered that; what would he have done, if he had proved this, and not simply that?" Or by interrogation: "What is there that has not been proved?" or, "What has my opponent proved?" We may, therefore, either sum up by comparison, or in the natural order of the statements, just as they were made, our own first, and then again, separately, if we so desire, what has been said by our opponent.

[6] To the conclusion of the speech the most appropriate style is that which has no connecting particles, in order that it may be a peroration, but not an oration: "I have spoken; you have heard; you know the facts; now give your decision."

Printed in Great Britain
by Amazon

40459374R00066